ROMAN IMPERIALISM IN THE LATE REPUBLIC

ROMAN IMPERIALISM IN THE LATE REPUBLIC

By E. BADIAN

CORNELL UNIVERSITY PRESS
ITHACA · NEW YORK

First published in the United States in 1968

Library of Congress Catalog Card Number: 68-8998

PRINTED IN ENGLAND

PREFACE TO THE FIRST EDITION

THESE lectures were delivered at a vacation school in Ancient History organised by the University of South Africa in July 1965. At the kind suggestion of the University, they are here published much as delivered. Simple annotation has been added, and I should like to thank the University for allowing me the space for this. It should suffice to draw the attention of the reader not expert in the subject to the main sources and to modern discussions where more can be found. The text of the lectures has not, on the whole, been much changed: the only consistent adaptation has been an attempt to eliminate that *ubertas* which—necessary if the listener is to follow the spoken word—becomes an irritant in print. As the revision was completed in December 1965, it was possible to insert at least some references to relevant work that had appeared by that date.

I should like to thank all those colleagues who discussed points arising out of the lectures with me at Pretoria: especially Professors W. den Boer and C. P. T. Naudé, who, while busy with their own contributions to the occasion, found time to improve mine; Professors G. van N. Viljoen and H. L. Gonin, who asked many searching questions with exemplary courtesy; and also Professor Mary White, of Toronto, who, on a short visit to England, was kind enough to read the typescript. They have all helped to make what is necessarily a sketchy treatment of an important subject a little less defective.

But it is my chief duty and pleasure to thank my South African colleagues, both at the University of South Africa and at other universities and colleges (most of which I visited), for unfailing and—what is rarer still—self-effacing hospitality. Amid the problems facing their country (which are obvious indeed, though to the historian no more so than those of countries less aware of their own), it was gratifying to find an interest in Classical studies, and indeed in civilised traditions in general, which, if there is any value in those traditions, cannot fail to play its part in solving the problems.

E. Badian

University of Leeds, England
December 1965

INTRODUCTION TO THE SECOND EDITION

WHEN the first edition of this book—a few hundred copies, published in a University of South Africa series—was reported to be out of print, Sir Basil Blackwell kindly took charge of publishing it in a slightly revised form, thus adding to the many *beneficia* for which I owe him gratitude. Though there has not yet been time for reviews that could be taken into account, various friends have made helpful comments that have enabled me to improve substance or style. I should especially like to mention Dr G. W. Bowersock and Dr E. S. Gruen.

I have made no changes that would alter the basic nature of the book or remove it too far from the series of lectures as actually delivered. Since modern documentation has in any case been kept to a minimum, there has been no need for frantic attempts to bring it up to date. The only important work bearing on the subject that has appeared since the end of 1965 is C. Nicolet, *L'Ordre équestre à l'Epoque républicaine* (1966), supplying, at last, part of the long-needed treatment the Equites the absence of which I had noted. This is clearly not the place for a full discussion of that massive work. I am happy to see that Nicolet's detailed investigation has independently led him to many of the same conclusions at which I myself had arrived, on the economic and social basis of the *ordo*, on its interests and on its relations with the Senate. If he is right in his main thesis on the definition of the *ordo* (i.e., that the 'public horse' was essential to it), as I am inclined to think he is, we shall have to change our terminology in specialist works on the period down to Sulla: I have always regarded the use of the term 'Equites' in a wider sense as (for that period) proleptic (see my references to them in *FC*). However, as far as the period after

Sulla is concerned (and particularly that after the last successful censorship in 70), it seems to me that Nicolet has done nothing to invalidate the common use of the term in modern writers: his attempt to find an association between the men explicitly called 'equites' and the public horse for this period is a complete failure (see his pp. 189–192); and his final conclusion (p. 744) is only that the allusion to the public horse belongs essentially to the second century and 'rien n'indique que les autres ne l'aient pas possédé'! In fact, in the post-Sullan age, there was clearly no recognised way of either acquiring equestrian status (since there was no effective censorship and the parade of the cavalry had fallen into disuse), or, correspondingly, of stopping anyone with sufficient wealth and influence from claiming it. Provided he was free-born, no man of substance would easily be denied that dignified title. It follows that there is, for this age, no reason for changing the now traditional terminology.

The decision is more difficult for the age between C. Gracchus and Sulla. Nicolet's treatment of the *Lex Repetundarum* is perhaps the least satisfactory part of his book, both in language and sense and from the strictly epigraphical point of view (which, in fact, is not considered at all). Until that work is done again, it will probably be impossible to decide which of the two possible definitions of the class of *iudices* (by wealth or by equestrian status) should be adopted. For the moment, the definition by wealth (a census of 400,000 HS, as is—despite Nicolet's contention to the contrary—the usual opinion of modern scholars) seems to me far the more probable: precisely because the *Gracchani iudices*, during the period down to Sulla, do *not* seem to have been described as *equites Romani*. Pliny's confused, but noteworthy, exposition (*n.h.* xxxiii 34), and the very fact of the wide extension of the term in the last generation of the Republic and of its close connection with the *ordo* of *publicani*, seems to make this *prima facie* the more likely solution, especially if Nicolet's attempt to date the law obliging senators to return the horse after the Gracchan legislation is rejected—as it surely must be, in the light of the well-known allusion to it in Cicero's *de republica* and Cicero's equally well-known care to avoid anachronism. If the qualification for enrolment on the jury panel was possession of the public horse, and senators by definition did not possess the public horse, their specific exclusion from the panel does not appear to make sense; for we cannot in this instance (as in many others) operate with the concept of tralatician clauses, since this new definition of the panel was in fact one of the main points of the Gracchan law.

I have set this out at some length in order to justify my decision (not taken lightly) to make no change in my terminology regarding the equestrian order in consequence of Nicolet's work. The 'proleptic' use of the title 'Equites' for the *Gracchani iudices*, based on Cicero's usage from the point of view of his own generation, will continue to have advantages from the point of view of historical exposition, even if (as I now more than ever believe) it is not strictly accurate between C. Gracchus and Sulla. Meanwhile we must all wait for Nicolet's promised prosopography, and for further and more expert work on the text of the *Lex Repetundarum*.

Since the first edition went to press, Christian Meier's book *Res Publica Amissa* has also appeared (Wiesbaden 1966). I hope to present my views on it in detail elsewhere. Here I would only note that, in what is relevant to the subject of these lectures, the views he expresses are very close to mine, especially on the aims and the role of the Equites in general and the *publicani* in particular (pp. 64–95); though it will be clear that we diverge on the apportionment of blame for the disintegration of the *res publica*.

Buffalo, N.Y.
  October 1967

CONTENTS

ABBREVIATIONS

Periodicals are abbreviated as in *L'Année philologique*, with slight simplifications that will cause no difficulty.

The following standard reference works are abbreviated in the usual manner:

FIRA[2]	*Fontes Iuris Romani Anteiustiniani*, 2nd ed. (ed. Riccobono)
ILLRP	*Inscriptiones Latinae Liberae Rei Publicae* (ed. Degrassi)
MRR	*The Magistrates of the Roman Republic* (ed. Broughton)
OGIS	*Orientis Graeci Inscriptiones Selectae* (ed. Dittenberger)
ORF[3]	*Oratorum Romanorum Fragmenta*, 3rd ed. (ed. Malcovati)
RE	Pauly-Wissowa-Kroll, *Real-Encyclopaedie der klassischen Altertumswissenschaft*
SIG[3]	*Sylloge Inscriptionum Graecarum*, 3rd ed. (ed. Dittenberger)

The following works are abbreviated as shown:

Frank, *ESAR*	T. Frank, *Economic Survey of Ancient Rome* (i, 1933)
Frank, *RI*	T. Frank, *Roman Imperialism* (1925)
Rostovtzeff, *SEHHW*	M. Rostovtzeff, *Social and Economic History of the Hellenistic World* (1941)
Rostovtzeff, *SEHRE*[2]	M. Rostovtzeff, *Social and Economic History of the Roman Empire*, 2nd ed. (ed. P. M. Fraser, 1957)

Naturally, I have had to rely on my own past work and, to save space (and not through any arrogant desire to put myself on a level with the preceding works), have abbreviated my own books as follows:

FC	*Foreign Clientelae (264–70 B.C.)* (1958)
SGRH	*Studies in Greek and Roman History* (1964)

VIRTVS AND *IMPERIVM*

IMPERIALISM[1] in some sense is as old as the human race, or at least as its social organisation. The extension of power by one's own group over others is only a special case of the victory of one's own side over others: in human terms, it does not call for an explanation. The naive joy in this that we find in Victorian imperialists or (for that matter) in a modern football crowd is as obvious in Cicero, with his numerous proud references to the glory and the victories of the Roman People—which are almost the only serious ideas he developed in public about the theory and practice of politics beyond his own community!

What does call for an explanation, when it appears in history, is that relatively high level of sophistication that *rejects* opportunities for the extension of power. As in the curbing of private ambition, either or both of two motives may lead to this: we may call them considerations of expediency or morality—in Roman terms, the *utile* and the *honestum*. The individual may realise that the pursuit of his ambition may be bad for his health or happiness; or he may come to question the principle of competition and the pursuit of power and distinction as a motive force. Similarly the community. We are not going to be concerned with the *merits* of this: in the first case one may speak of prudence or pusillanimity, in the second of saintliness or neurotic decadence. Our point is only that both these motives, in their different ways, are signs of sophistication, overcoming the deep-seated urge for domination and power.

Policy at Rome, as we all now know,[2] was in practice determined by a governing oligarchy, which reached its zenith in the second century B.C. Its attitude to our question was a highly complex one. It had long outgrown the most primitive stage: indeed, as Mommsen recognised long ago,[3] most of the second century is characterised by a highly sophisticated policy of avoiding annexation. In the West, Carthage had been left standing in 201, and its chances of future prosperity little diminished. In the East, Philip V of Macedon had been defeated by 196 and a decision of principle had to be taken. Titus Quinctius Flamininus, combining the methods of Roman with the lessons of Greek history (which he will certainly have known), convinced the Senate that Rome must appear as the liberator of the Greeks while pursuing what was in effect her traditional policy.[4] So the 'freedom of the Greeks' was proclaimed in a theatrical scene at the Isthmian Games of 196; and though there was strong pressure among cautious senators for the military occupation of at least some key fortresses in Greece, Flamininus in the end overcame it and, after the war with Nabis of Sparta, withdrew all the Roman troops. The decision had been taken and was not reversed, despite the opposition of the great Scipio. Indeed, against the threat of advance by Antiochus III, Rome (under Flamininus' direction) intensified its propaganda efforts to appear as the champion of Greek freedom against enslavement to kings and oppression. Once Antiochus had been defeated, this line proved unprofitable and was abandoned: in their cold-blooded attitude over this, the Romans showed, to all who would observe, their contempt of foreign opinion when it no longer mattered. To leave all the Greeks free would have led to anarchy, while Rome now wanted order. But the principle of non-annexation was preserved—indeed, the very desire for order shows its strength: Rome wanted to be sure she would not have to intervene again. Eumenes of Pergamum and (to a lesser extent) the Republic of Rhodes received large increases of territory and became the protagonists of the Roman order in Asia. In Europe, Macedon was left intact, though not allowed to expand in Greece; and the Greeks continued without supervision. It is clear that the Senate hoped they would be able to run their own affairs, taking its advice, as loyal clients, when it was asked for or offered.

Indeed, this did not work out as planned: during the next generation, as one party after another kept appealing to Rome, and the clients ignored advice frequently given but never backed by force, the Senate—against its will, clearly—was drawn more and more into perpetual intervention, both to keep order and to restore its fading prestige. Yet the fact is that down to the war with Perseus, and again after it, no Roman governor or soldier was stationed east of the Adriatic, despite the astonishing successes that Roman arms had won as far to the east as Mount Taurus, and the equally astonishing failure to have Roman wishes in Greece consistently carried out.

When Macedon became more powerful and began to intrigue among the Greek states, the Senate—rightly or wrongly—came to the conclusion that another war would have to be fought. Questionable diplomacy was used;[5] yet in the end there was again no annexation. The Aegean world after the battle of Pydna looked a very different place from what it had been before. The kingdom of Macedon was broken up into its four traditional constituent districts, which were made into separate 'free' states.[6] A thousand Achaeans, among them Polybius, were deported to Italy, and no doubt numbers of Greeks from other states. Rhodes was left humbled and its naval power broken. Pergamum had fallen into disfavour and was thrown open to attacks by hostile neighbours. Roman interference in Asia as in Europe had become open and undisguised, leaving no strong power anywhere to keep order as before. Yet it was still true that not a single Roman governor or soldier stood east of the Adriatic. Methods had changed; but the principles had remained, and indeed become even more obvious. The overriding aim, as before, was to avoid annexation (which, in terms of power, could easily have been imposed). The first method tried had been to leave one or two strong powers to keep order: they had become too strong and were thus felt to be dangerous to Rome. Now the only alternative that might achieve the aim was tried: weakness and fragmentation, with constant inspection—even at the risk of anarchy. But the assumption of

3

direct responsibility was not even considered. Rome might still claim that her purpose was merely to ensure peace and prevent threats to her safety.

Yet, clearly, this is only half the picture. Nothing could be further from the truth than to suppose that the Roman oligarchy felt a moral repugnance towards aggression and domination or believed in the co-existence of equal and fully sovereign states. Indeed, to the last century of the Republic, the censors by custom had to pray to the gods for an increase in the possessions of the Roman people.[7] Whether or not individual Roman nobles ever seriously believed that the threat of foreign powers was necessary to maintain the soundness of the Roman body politic—a view that, even if P. Scipio Nasica did in fact express it in opposition to the elder Cato, was blown up into a political principle only *ex post facto*—there is no doubt that such a view never provided a basis of action for the Roman state as such.[8] Roman policy in Greece early in the century, and in the Aegean area as a whole after 167, shows a mixture of petulance and arrogance that, despite its failure to obtain obedience to Roman wishes in detail, was only too successful in perpetuating intrigue and tension and preventing the emergence of any strong power. Non-annexation, in fact, never meant non-intervention.

Roman imperialism can therefore still be said to have existed in the East; but it was not of the annexationist kind: it was of what we may call the 'hegemonial' kind.[9] On the barbarian fringe of the Empire, on the other hand, war never stopped. In Spain, Liguria or Sardinia no settled frontier ever existed. For decades slow conquest, interrupted by many setbacks, gradually expanded the occupied and pacified zone. We hear few details of all these operations, except in a handful of spectacular cases: they were taken for granted.[10] Hence, though the facts are obvious enough, their significance is easily overlooked. Yet both the similarities and the differences between Roman policy towards civilised and towards barbarian states are striking. We must come back to them later.

It might be thought that the failure to admit the independent existence of other powers and their right to run their affairs without intervention from outside was due to the spirit of the age—a tradition from which Rome merely failed to escape. Yet this does not seem to have been so. Whatever had been the case in Classical Greece (and it was perhaps not so very different from what followed), a concert of Hellenistic powers had existed for a century, when Rome so violently intruded upon it. The principal Hellenistic states, while often engaged in wars over contested territories and in intrigues to undermine one another's influence, seem, after two generations of anarchy following the death of Alexander the Great, to have recognised an equilibrium on the general maintenance of which the independent existence of each of them was based. The Ptolemies, the Seleucids, the Antigonids, as well as smaller powers like Pergamum, Bithynia or even the Aetolian and Achaean Leagues—they all had their part to play, and the disappearance of any of them would have led to a major catastrophe. Very probably, this was merely a recognition of the limitations of the various Hellenistic powers—it was based purely on expediency.[11] But it was nevertheless effective in recreating a relatively stable world in the third century. The Hellenistic world, like that of modern Europe for centuries before the Great War, was one based on a balance that, as each power knew, had to be preserved at least in essentials.

Roman policy, from almost as far back as we can trace it, was different. Of course, for a long time Rome had to recognise the equality of some other powers: thus in the early treaties with Carthage recorded by Polybius.[12] Indeed, before 218 B.C. she could hardly have *denied* equality to Carthage or to the great powers of the East. But right from the start there was the determination to dominate whatever was within reach and to build up strength to extend that reach. Equality was conceded only beyond the range of effective power, and every attempt was made to build up power where it had shown itself deficient. It is clear that the Romans always ended up by heavily outnumbering their rivals.[13] By the middle of the fourth century, hegemony had been claimed over Latium, while the Samnites were an equal enemy—or (as in the Latin War) ally. By the time of the war with Pyrrhus, the whole of Italy was claimed as a hegemonial sphere,[14] and victory justified the claim. By the end of the twenties it had been extended to the adjacent islands and to territories across the Ionian and Adriatic Seas. Within the areas thus staked out, independent states were, after a fashion, permitted and even encouraged to exist: like the many Italian states with their different treaties, or the kingdoms and free cities of Sicily and Illyria.[15] But, whatever the exact status of those communities, in what Rome regarded as essential—their foreign policy—they were effectively under Roman control. The state of affairs that we found so characteristic of Roman policy in the second century, and so surprising in its Hellenistic context, had always been the same, as far as Rome was concerned.

On two occasions, as Rome came into contact with the Hellenistic concert of powers, it looked for a moment as though she might adopt its standards and fit her different traditions and organisation into that Greek world that so obviously attracted her leading citizens. First, in the Peace of Phoenice (205 B.C.) it seems a genuine attempt was made to secure co-existence on equal terms with Philip V by leaving an insulating layer of buffer states between the two powers. Had this succeeded, Rome might have stopped there (as far as the East was concerned)—at least long enough to become pervaded with the new concept of a polity and a balance of states. But Philip, over-confident, began to interfere with the buffer states in Illyria while at the same time extending his power in the East. The causes of the Second Macedonian War have been interminably discussed. It is clear that it was in fact due to Roman suspicion of Philip's successes and ambitious policies on various fronts, seen against the background of his 'stab in the back' in the Hannibalic War. But I have elsewhere tried to bring out—certainly not as the only, but as a very obvious cause—what is indeed obvious in Livy's account: the breakdown of the

Illyrian settlement, at the only point where the two powers met and directly clashed. An attempt had been made at Phoenice to secure peace: but Philip had made it impossible. The result was the war that established Roman hegemony over Greece and Macedonia.[16]

The next turning-point came when, at a secret conference in Rome, Titus Quinctius Flamininus faced the envoys of Antiochus III and made them an offer in terms of cold-blooded geopolitics, contrasting with his carefully developed public propaganda position: if the King kept out of Europe, Rome would keep out of Asia. There is no reason to doubt that he—and the Senate—meant it. But again an Eastern king, over-confident in his strength, refused to settle.[17] The result was the war that ended at Magnesia and Apamea. Henceforth—at least until the Parthians were seen to be dangerous—there were no equals left. Rome never again behaved as if there were.

The puzzling contradiction in Roman policy—open aggression and expansionism against barbarians; hegemonial imperialism with careful avoidance of annexation towards cultural equals or superiors—this peculiar adaptation of the urge for domination that underlies them both cannot, of course, be exhaustively explained, any more than any other phenomenon of any importance and complexity in historical enquiry. But there are some clues we should follow. First, it became clear to the Roman governing class at an early stage that large increases of territory could not easily be administered within the existing city-state constitution. Rather than change the latter—which was inconceivable, though minor adaptations (such as the promagistracy) were freely tried—annexation was, on the whole, soon abandoned for subordination by treaty. With power expanding beyond Italy, even this became too burdensome, since it imposed definite and often inconvenient commitments on Rome. Hence the further step towards the 'free' ally, city or king, controlled without a treaty. It must be confessed that under the Roman Republic no real system of administering overseas territories was ever evolved: those that were annexed (like most of Sicily and Sardinia) were merely the allotted spheres of action (*prouinciae*) of a military commandant (at first normally a praetor) who, right until the end of the Republic, governed under what was not far removed from a permanent (though slightly regularised) state of siege. But that is another story.[18] Meanwhile we must notice that, down to the middle of the second century, all but one of the provinces remained active theatres of war—rich in triumphs, but costly to the state. Sicily was probably the only one that regularly realised a surplus for the Treasury. The rest were a constant drain in money—and, worse still, in manpower. Rome and Italy could hardly cope with the demand.[19] Small wonder, therefore, that the Senate was slow to start major wars when it could be avoided—and certainly not for the sake of annexation, which, more often than not, proved merely a prelude to a future of minor wars.

Moreover, early in the second century the Scipios had given a terrible warning to the majority of their peers. Adopting names to represent the *orbis terrarum* they claimed to have conquered (Africanus, Asiaticus, Hispallus), they had threatened—not indeed a military tyranny, as some later Romans thought and some modern authors still hanker after saying: for this was quite inconceivable at the time—no, they had threatened to acquire an overpowering prestige that might make the egalitarian working of oligarchic government practically impossible. The Scipios had gone down to defeat; but their example remained, and the lesson was learnt: great overseas commands were carefully avoided.[20]

There is another point to consider. We shall have to say some harsh things about the Senate in due course; but let us give praise where it is due. It is all the more necessary to stress that it looks as if concern over standards of magistrates' behaviour in the provinces was another powerful influence in discouraging annexation and its consequence, direct administration. There was trouble quite early: in 171 B.C. major complaints came from Spain about the actions of governors there. Not much was done: some of the men were well connected.[21] The Roman oligarchy, like other oligarchies, was reluctant to punish its members for the sake of its subjects. There was more trouble in the fifties.[22] The excessive powers enjoyed by the holders of *imperium* were bound to corrupt. What is more, they led to an excess of pride and individualism—for which Hellenistic cultural influence often gets the blame. This would make men stand out against the Senate. Livy offers many examples of disobedient magistrates at the height of the Senate's power. Some succeeded in their designs or at least went unpunished: it was never easy to exercise effective control. Nor could the mercurial popular assembly be relied on for a responsible judgment.[23] There can be no doubt that these considerations weighed heavily with the Senate as a whole in its set policy of minimising overseas commitments.

It is significant that the first serious attempt to deal with the problem of misbehaviour in the provinces comes in 149.[24] In that year L. Calpurnius Piso, the virtuous tribune surnamed Frugi, passed the first law that was to enable oppressed allies at least to get back what they had lost. A permanent *quaestio repetundarum* was set up, to take the place of the all too frequent *ad hoc* commissions of the Senate for this purpose. There were no severe penalties (if there were any), for the time being.[25] Rightly, one is inclined to think. It became only too clear in the later Republic that severe extortion laws merely made senatorial juries (and not only them) more unwilling to convict, and more amenable to the sort of appeal for sympathy for a Roman senator against wretched foreigners at which Cicero (when it suited him) was such a master. Piso's law seems to have provided merely for restitution. Obviously, it was really meant to work. Now, what is most significant about it, perhaps, is its date. For in 149 the war against Carthage had started, and it is clear that the Senate was beginning to realise that this time there was no solution short of annexation. In the same year, the praetor P. Iuventius Thalna was defeated by the pretender Andriscus, who had united Macedonia (which the Romans had divided up) against the settlement of 167.[26] Again, it is reasonable to think that the Senate knew that another experiment in non-annexation had failed. It is therefore interesting—and to the credit of the Fathers—that precisely in that year, with large-scale further annexation imminent and inevitable, they made an honest attempt to protect their subjects against the worst effects of misbehaviour on the part of magistrates. The Senate as a whole—as it was to show as late as 95, when it sent Q. Mucius Scaevola to Asia,[27] not to mention 72, when the consuls proposed a decree at least trying to curb Verres[28]—the Senate, in 149 as at other times, took its responsibilities seriously. This gives us the right of positing such considerations as among the motives for the avoidance of annexation.

As far as the Hellenistic East is concerned, an important political consideration may be added. Early in the second century T. Flamininus discovered what monarchs had known for generations: the power of Greek public opinion. Gradually he converted the Senate to his views. Political hegemony in the East traditionally depended on at least a modicum of co-operation. Hence relations with at least some of the kings, leagues and cities were—most of the time—carefully watched, to secure and retain the approval of those who mattered. It was a civilised and interconnected world, where—as in ours—political actions at once received vast publicity. This had to be considered; and the war against Perseus, with its vicissitudes, made it even clearer. Very different was the situation on the barbarian 'frontier': there no one (except perhaps a man's *inimici*, for their private profit) greatly cared what was done to a Ligurian or Iberian tribe. The record of Roman war and policy in Spain—as, in particular, A. Schulten insisted[29]—is one of cruelty and treachery almost unparalleled in Roman history. Yet not a single commander came to serious harm as a result: not the perfidious mass murderer Ser. Sulpicius Galba,[30] whom Cato tried to attack, but who survived to be an honoured master of Roman oratory; nor C. Hostilius Mancinus, who made a treaty with the Numantines which he probably knew the Senate would dishonour: handed over to them, naked and bound, in expiation, he found (as he had no doubt expected) that the barbarians were far too humane to punish him; whereupon he returned to Rome, was allowed to resume his citizenship and soon rose to be praetor again.[31]

Thus a double standard of behaviour developed. In the East, a hegemonial policy was pursued in a cautious and, on the whole, fairly civilised way, at least without violence and open treachery and certainly (as long as it proved possible) without direct control and major wars. But against the barbarians, where publicity need not be feared and where, incidentally, the gradual advancing of the frontier did not, on the whole, lead to any major new commitment at any one time, so that the whole process would not easily become obvious—there policy was openly brutal and aggressive, and triumph-hunting an accepted technique.

Of course, in this distinction in what was permitted towards barbarians and what towards Hellenes (i.e., at this time, civilised states) the Romans were fitting themselves into a Greek tradition that went back a long time. In Greece it can be demonstrated as early as the fifth century;[32] while in Roman policy, as late as the First Macedonian War, there is no sign of such a distinction.[33] And so, even if tales of Roman behaviour in the West did filter through to Greek cities, the Romans had nothing to fear: it is doubtful whether anyone other than a few philosophers cared. As for the principle of fetial law, that no war was acceptable to the gods unless it was waged in defence of one's own country or one's allies —whether this applied to native tribes is not quite certain; though in theory it probably did.[34] But, as is well known, the law was by now a mere ritual, robbed of all real content. The Romans had quite early developed a standard technique for evading ritual pollution: to make an alliance with a state exposed to certain attack and to defend it when the attack came. A variant of this can be observed, with a further loosening of the legal element, in the ultimatum that preceded the Second Macedonian War.[35] But in the second century, though it is possible that the ritual was still performed—perhaps even as late as the Jugurthine War[36]—none of our sources pays the slightest attention to it, and as far as its motive power in policy is concerned, we must clearly follow them and ignore it.

As we have seen, the double standard of behaviour yet went back to a single basic attitude. Both the bellicose annexationism and the hegemonial policy spring from deeply rooted features of Roman life. It is these that we must now briefly consider.

The values of Roman aristocratic life were those characteristic of that form of society.[37] High birth and merit (*genus* and *uirtus*) were chiefly admired. The former—descent from distinguished ancestors—was taken to be a *prima facie* guarantee of the latter, imposing both a standard and a challenge. The latter (*uirtus*) was the real touchstone of achievement and the only claim that could be advanced by the 'new man', who lacked the guarantee of high birth. The aristocratic poet Lucilius, at the end of a long passage full of high-sounding Greek sentiment, defined it in a few simple words: 'commoda patriai prima putare'. *Virtus* as an aristocratic Roman concept has been much discussed. It has even been suggested that originally the term meant a primitive magic power, a kind of *mana*, which naturally inhered in leading men.[38] This meaning, if it ever existed, was, of course, much changed by the second century, particularly as Greek philosophy began to affect Roman education. But the quality was always most fully embodied in the commander and statesman: it was very much a *public* virtue, and one of the ruling class—at least, as seen by that class. Its chief example was, as we have seen, the man who, having the deeds of great ancestors as a model, administered the state in war and peace to its greatest advantage. The Roman aristocracy was always conscious of its destiny.

What really counted, by the second century, is perhaps best seen in the famous epitaphs of the Scipios.[39] It was—if one ignored a few Greek ideas that, as Lucilius' poetic discussion shows, did not count for so very much in the practical test—descent, offices and military success.

L. Cornelius Scipio Barbatus (consul 298 B.C.) boasts that his *forma uirtutei parisuma fuit* (thus making his bow to Greek admiration for beauty, but clearly distinguishing it from Roman *uirtus*). He goes on, in a very Roman way, to give proof of his *uirtus*, which is clearly what really counts: he gives his offices (*consol censor aidilis quei fuit apud uos*) and finally his great deeds in war (*Taurasia Cisaunia Samnio cepit, subigit omne Loucanam opsidesque abdoucit*). Barbatus' son (consul 259) claims to be, by common consent, the best man of all Romans (*duonoro optumo fuise uiro*). Again he illustrates this with his offices (consulate, censorship, aedileship) and his victories (*hec cepet Corsica Aleriaque urbe*); finally he cites his *pietas* in dedicating a temple, thus bringing in a religious element that is surprisingly rare elsewhere. But most eloquent, perhaps, is the epitaph of a young L. Scipio, a son of the great Asiaticus, who died as a quaestorian of 33 and thus had no chance of demonstrating his *uirtus* in command and high administration. He proudly claims: *pater regem Antioco subegit*. At least he could be proud of his father's *uirtus*.

Military success and the holding of office: these are the chief claims to *uirtus*. Within the aristocracy, as we all know, Roman politics, especially in the second century B.C., was a constant struggle for prestige (*dignitas*), pursued with single-minded ambition. It was a highly competitive society. But this prestige, as we have seen even from contemporary evidence, found its chief support in the holding of office and in military success. This requisite glory had to be gathered somewhere. And since in the second century major wars, and wars against civilised states, were (as we have found) on the whole against public policy, it had to be gathered on the barbarian frontier. There it would not commit the State (at least at any one time) to more than it could undertake; it would not endanger Rome's public reputation; and the successes gained would not be so overpowering as to arouse fear and *inuidia* among a man's peers. Triumphs were essential to the Roman way of life and politics; and it is not surprising that triumph-hunting against barbarians became a recognised pursuit—a matter of political life or death to many a Roman noble. Even in the first century, a man's refusal to indulge in it could be used by an enemy to attack his character and damn his reputation.⁴⁰

The other aspect—the hegemonial policy—goes back to an equally characteristic tradition of the Roman aristocracy: that of patronage. From the very start of Roman history, powerful men had had free 'clients' attached to their persons and families. These men, though legally free, were by custom—and by the facts of power—obliged to obey and serve their patron in return for his protection. In a wider sense of the word, every *beneficium* created a relation of clientship, obliging the recipient to be prepared to render *officia*. Naturally, the ability to confer *beneficia* was, on the whole, also an aristocratic privilege; so that, in addition to their direct dependants, upper-class individuals and families were surrounded by a circle of others whom they had placed under an obligation and who were expected to repay them on demand.⁴¹

It was in this way, to a large extent, that the oligarchy maintained its power for so long in the Roman state; and it was in this way that rivals fought each other for office and prestige: indeed, the latter was, to a certain extent, visibly measured by the number of clients a man could muster. Inevitably, these relationships spread beyond the city of Rome and its territory, as Rome came into contact with places and peoples more and more remote—first to Italy, then to the provinces, 'free' cities and even neighbouring monarchs. Both collectively and as individuals, men abroad owed *officia* to the Roman aristocrats who had conferred *beneficia* on them, e.g. by governing them, by sparing them after victory, by looking after their interests in Rome. It was a natural consequence that Roman aristocrats, accustomed to seeing personal relationships, both within the community and outside, in these terms of moral relationships and duties based (ultimately) on the facts of power, should transfer this attitude to their political thinking: that Rome, in fact, should appear as the patron city, claiming the *officia* both of actual allies and subjects and of 'free' kings and cities with which she had come into contact. These attitudes were woven into the Roman noble's life. Of course, it was the oligarchy, acting

14

through the Senate, that represented Rome—the patronal power —in its relations with those clients, thus reinforcing the bonds of individual clientship that personally united many of them to great Roman houses. It was clear that the whole world owed *officia* to the great power acting through the men who governed it. As Roman power increased, it became impossible, for those brought up under this system, to see any relationship between Romans and foreigners, between Rome and foreign states, in other terms than these; and this explains what often—by our standards—seems arrogance and even naïveté in Roman behaviour. The obedience of the weak to the strong was, to the Roman aristocrat, nothing less than an eternal moral law.

THE 'ECONOMIC MOTIVE'

I HAVE been trying to relate the complex nature of Roman imperialism, as it is found in the second century B.C., to the nature and the conventions of Roman aristocratic society. In every society, there is inevitably a close connection between the values and way of life—the *Weltanschauung*—of the leading classes of that society at home and the way in which the society, as led by those classes, will act in its foreign relations. This is particularly so where, as in the case of Rome, a small and relatively isolated society has, within a very few generations, found its horizons vastly extended, almost to the limits of the civilised world of its time; and where, moreover, it has entered that world as a superior and a master, able to make others to a very large extent conform to its own patterns. We shall see later that, at a different stage of social and international development, the influence could go the other way and the relations of eminent Romans with most of the outside world could impose a pattern on internal relationships. But at the point we have reached that was still in the future, even though dimly visible. The constant interaction of the internal temper and customs of social life and the external environment of a society is an important and obvious field of study to the historian trying to evaluate both. Yet these aspects are often studied in isolation and thus individually distorted.

The modern student, accustomed to seeing history—at least at at second or at tenth hand—through the blood-red spectacles of Marx, may by now have become impatient with my approach, observing that a discussion of Roman imperialism in terms of politics, strategy, social *ethos* and even psychology, surely misses the point: what (he will say) about revenues, markets, exports? These (we are constantly taught) are the real stuff of imperialism.

This view is not confined to the student unfamiliar with the evidence. Variants of it have at times been propounded by distinguished scholars:[1] we shall never escape contemporary fashions, and economic explanations of political events are commonly supposed to be one of the distinctively modern contributions to historical research. Yet this seems to me an obvious case where we tend to see history through distorting spectacles. I shall not follow up the larger question of whether such views, even in the case of our own society and the more recent past, tend to give an inadequate and distorted explanation of historical events: though I would not deny the importance of economic motives for political actions, it seems to me clear that this importance can vary considerably in different conditions and even in different cases, and that failure to recognise this, and over-emphasis on economic factors, has led, not only to many mistaken historical interpretations, but also to many wrong political decisions. However, our main point at present is that no such motives can be seen, on the whole, in Roman policy, during the period that we are now considering.

Naturally, we have one or two cases of economic privileges secured for Romans and Italians: the best-known is freedom from duty at Ambracia.[2] There is also that old favourite of economic historians, the free harbour established at Delos in 167 B.C.[3] However, those directly benefiting (particularly in the latter case) were not Roman aristocrats—though these may have got the odd slave a little more cheaply—nor even, to a large extent, Roman citizens: apart from numerous Syrians and other Orientals, they were Italians. Many of the 'Romans' at Delos come from Oscan Italy.[4] The protecting power, acting in the true spirit of a patron, was mindful of *beneficia* to confer—at no cost to itself—on its loyal allies. For in Italy the freedom and dignity of the Italian allies—whom moderns sometimes still miscall the 'Italian Confederacy'[5]—had been mortally wounded by the Hannibalic War and the

17

two decades of disturbances that followed. Roman arrogance and lack of respect for the independence of the allies—whatever their treaty rights—were becoming painfully evident. But the Senate as a whole, though it could not always control its members, and though it might at times not be unwilling to make Roman power perfectly plain in the Peninsula, carefully fulfilled the obligations imposed by superior *uirtus*. And the upper class of Italy was, on the whole, satisfied. There is no sign of serious discontent, no demand for equality (not to mention citizenship), until Roman demagogues, for their own purposes connected with internal politics, create it in the 120s.[6] Had the Senate not fulfilled its obligations— on the whole—to its clients' satisfaction, the Social War would have come much sooner and would perhaps have ended differently. Politics and even economics must be seen in their Roman aristocratic context.

Strange as it may seem to a generation nourished on Marx, Rome sought no major economic benefits. In their four provinces, the Romans simply went on collecting—with as little readjustment as possible—the tribute those regions had paid to their previous masters, the Carthaginians or their own king. Even the methods of collection, left essentially unchanged, brought little profit to Roman *publicani*. Of course, the Romans were too prudent in matters financial to give up established revenues; but they kept them as much from inertia as from conscious choice, and mostly because the alternative was simply inconceivable. It is unlikely (as we have seen) that at this time any province was even paying its way, except for peaceful and prosperous Sicily. In Macedonia, in 167, the royal mines were for a time closed down, to avoid throwing them open to Roman speculators:[7] the motive has been questioned and Livy arraigned; but since the fact can hardly be denied, it is difficult to find any other plausible motive for such a thoroughly un-Roman action. The tribute that the four regions of Macedon had paid to their king was halved when they became independent republics. Perhaps it would have been unreasonable to demand the full amount from those weakened states. But exploiters would hardly stop to think of this. In fact, the tribute was perhaps imposed—as Frank pointed out—to pay for the expenses of the war, which could not be charged to anyone else's account:[8] Rome had certainly come to feel that she should not, as victor, be expected to pay for her wars.

So much for exploitation. The wars themselves, of course, were highly profitable—especially the great Eastern wars. After the triumph of L. Paullus citizens had no more direct taxes to pay.[9] Money, slaves and works of art poured into the city.[10] This was the ancient law of war. No one would have dreamt of questioning it. But, as we have already had occasion to see, neither this nor anything else in fact made the Senate eager for great wars, especially in the rich East. The profits, when they came, were welcome and were taken as a matter of course. But they were not a motive for political and military action; they were not actively sought.

Finally, markets. In a well-known passage beloved of economic historians, Scipio Aemilianus is made by Cicero to reprove the Romans for not allowing Transalpine tribes to plant vines or olives, in order to make their own farms more profitable.[11] Rostovtzeff called this 'a prohibition on vine and olive culture in the Western provinces' and seized on it as his crowning demonstration of economic motives in Rome's foreign policy as early as 154 (or possibly 125) B.C.[12] In fact, as Tenney Frank had by then already pointed out,[13] and as Rostovtzeff would have seen, had he looked again at the text, the wording specifies the tribes of Transalpine Gaul, and thus *excludes* the other western provinces—such countries as Spain and Sicily, rich in vines and olives. What economic sense is there in that?

But there is, in fact, another consideration that damns this ill-conceived theory. We must remember that the *Republic*, where this passage occurs, has 129 B.C. as its dramatic date. Now, Roman treaties were kept in archives or even displayed in public, and Cicero certainly had access to the one that contained the provision he here attacked. So would those who mattered among his audience. It is inconceivable that he should here be guilty of a gross chronological blunder and refer to a treaty that was in fact dated *after* 129: even Rostovtzeff's alternative of 125 will not do. Had Cicero made the incredible mistake, his friend Atticus, that careful chronologer, would have corrected it.[14] A Roman aristocratic reading public did not permit the sort of pseudo-history that an Athenian orator could get away with in court. However, if the treaty concerned was already in existence in 129, it must belong to the campaign of 154—the only time before 129 when Rome had come into contact with Transalpine Gauls to an extent that could possibly involve such treaties. This campaign, as Tenney Frank stressed, had been entered into at the appeal of Massilia; and after its end, as far as we know, the Romans, for a full generation, continued to have no interest whatever in southern Gaul. They certainly did not own an acre of it, or have contacts close enough to lead to differences of opinion; and so Tenney Frank's explanation of the treaty Cicero saw is inevitable: the term he objects to must have been included at the request of Massilia, which itself had both agricultural and trading interests, and in fact probably almost a monopoly of trade in the area. We must only note, for future reference, that by Cicero's day, when the actual conditions of 154 had long been forgotten, and men judged—as men will judge—the past by the present, the interpretation that Cicero gives seemed the obvious one. The passage, therefore, is valuable evidence on his own day.

The whole myth of economic motives in Rome's foreign policy at this time is a figment of modern anachronism, based on ancient anachronism, like so many modern myths about the ancient world. Though exposed by Tenney Frank long ago, it is still from time to time fashionably reaffirmed; but it should be allowed to die. We must add, briefly, that the destruction of Carthage and Corinth, sometimes cited against Frank's thesis, in fact confirms it: having it in their power to settle on those splendid commercial sites (as, much later, they did), the Romans preferred to plough them up. Their motives were purely strategic and political: to strike at strongly fortified centres of traditional anti-Roman leadership.

We might compare the long hesitation over the foundation of a settlement at Capua.[15]

In fact, the events of 148–6 show the Senate's traditional policy and frame of mind. Macedonia had to be annexed, after controlled independence had turned out disastrous: the Romans, on the whole, never made the same mistake twice. The same—from the Roman point of view—applied to the small strip of Tunisia which was all that was left of Carthage and its empire.[16] But Greece, despite all the troubles her cities had caused, was, for the most part, still not put under direct administration; and a Greek—the historian Polybius—was left to work out the details of the final settlement.[17] In Africa, part of the small territory annexed was immediately handed over to the possession of loyal allied cities that remained 'free', i.e. outside the province.[18] So little did Rome care about the exploitation even of land that rightly belonged to her. (Or, if we prefer it, so seriously did the Senate still take the duties of patronage, to the neglect of Rome's economic interests.) The policy of minimising administrative commitments and caring little for profit derived from provincial territories could hardly appear more clearly.

And so it remained for the rest of the century. When Attalus III left his kingdom to Rome (quite without prompting, we may be sure, and following a precedent that Rome had almost certainly done nothing to create),[19] the Senate was not given a chance of discussing the strange bequest. We may well think that in some form it would have been accepted; but we cannot be sure even of that. As it happened, the tribune Tiberius Gracchus, through his hereditary connections with the royal house of Pergamum, heard of the testament first, and, needing money for his ambitious domestic schemes, he treated it as a windfall and passed a law in the Assembly accepting the inheritance and diverting the profits to his agrarian plans.[20] All this was done without consulting the Senate, even though this action was contrary to all precedent and bound to arouse strong opposition and the most serious alarm. In fact—a fact worth stressing, since it is easy to miss—it was his dealings with the Pergamene envoy that led immediately to the charge that Tiberius was aiming at a *regnum* and thus to his downfall.[21] That he omitted the obvious conciliatory step of consulting the Senate may in part have been due to his awareness of the personal antagonism he had by then aroused in it. But it is also conceivable that he was not at all sure that Senate policy would favour accepting the bequest he so urgently needed. Tiberius could not afford to take chances, if his scheme was not to be jeopardised.

Once the People had accepted the bequest, the step—in the political situation of the time—could not be reversed, and the Senate had to make the best of what it found. Forced to carry on Tiberius' actual scheme, it had to get the funds. As we shall see, this situation was not unique: it was to become a common setting for annexation and exploitation in the later Republic. Even so, it was decided to minimise commitments as far as possible. The cities of the kingdom were left 'free' (as Attalus had intended),[22] and five men were sent to Pergamum to organise the royal property on behalf of Rome. Their leader—ensuring that no irresponsible step was taken—was none other than the Pontifex Maximus P. Cornelius Scipio Nasica, Tiberius' chief enemy and murderer.[23] There would be no unnecessary annexation. In fact, what was done was probably much the same as later in Cyrene, when its king left it to Rome in 96: there the proper organisation of a province was not even begun until 75, and then only because disorder had become endemic and dangerous.[24] All that was done (inefficiently, it seems) was to arrange to draw some of the profits. That this policy was also pursued in 133 is—even in the absence of clear direct evidence—a legitimate and even necessary conjecture: in Rome, when an unusual situation arose, it was natural to consult *mos maiorum*; and in 96 there would still be senators alive who remembered—what the archives would in any case show—how a similar bequest had been dealt with in 133.

We may find confirmation in a small fact: the name of the province of Asia. When Aristonicus attempted to seize what he claimed was his inheritance, various Roman commanders were sent out to fight him—last of them M' Aquillius (*cos.* 129), who, as proconsul, completed the settlement.[25] Naturally, their *prouincia* for the war was *Asia*, as (e.g.) that of the Scipios had been against Antiochus.[26] Long before Sulla—in fact, as far back as we know— a Roman commander was not allowed to leave his *prouincia* without special permission: in 171, in a *cause célèbre*, a consul trying to do so had been peremptorily stopped by a Senate embassy.[27] Consequently, in a major war, the definition of the *prouincia* had to be wide and elastic, to ensure that the commander would be able to do his legitimate task without restriction. Hence 'Sicilia'. 'Africa', 'Asia' are allotted as *prouinciae*, even though those words embrace areas much wider than the probable scenes of action. As we have briefly seen, the Romans never evolved a system of civil provincial administration: the conditions of wartime were standardised and continued in adapted form. Hence the *prouinciae* of Sicilia, Africa or Asia became the provinces of Sicily, Africa and Asia—even though still much smaller than the areas to which the name concerned properly applied. Asia owed its name to its origin in a *prouincia*, not to a previous proclamation of annexation. We may compare and contrast Bithynia, duly annexed in 74[28] and left under that name (as part of a larger province) after its reoccupation. Had Attalus' kingdom been formally annexed in 133, we may well believe that its name would have been the province of Pergamum. In fact, there was—as so often—no annexation until revolt and disorder had made it inevitable. The province kept its military name.

Policy is, on the whole, similar in the West. While triumph-hunting (as we have seen) continues to perform its essential function in the domestic Roman political and social framework, and small-scale annexation is an inevitable consequence (e.g. in the Balearic Islands or in Illyria),[29] large opportunities for major expansion are ignored. A war in Transalpine Gaul, lasting from 125 until at least 120, with several commanders winning great victories, did not lead to the establishment of a province[30]—and that in an area where we are sometimes told the Romans had had a major interest thirty years earlier! The great road built by Cn. Domitius, meant to ensure—for the first time—land communications between Italy and Spain, was largely given over to Massilia to protect, with (perhaps) the help of a few small Roman garrisons.[31] Only years later—possibly as late as 115—when danger from the north became obvious, was a colony set up on the site of the settlement of Narbo Martius: a key site, *specula populi Romani ac propugnaculum* against the Gauls.[32] And this was done by the faction of Domitius himself, whose son became one of the founders of the colony; and it was done against the wishes of the Senate as a whole, which tried to deal with this colony as it had dealt with the Gracchan Junonia. Naturally, the colony was a *popularis causa*:[33] it called up memories of C. Gracchus' venture and many impoverished citizens could expect to settle there and to prosper. But—*pace* many modern scholars—there is no record of any interest in it on the part of the Equites, no record of anybody's being aware that it was an excellent commercial site, as our scholars are, and as Romans also were by the time of the early Empire.[34] And the argument is not merely one from silence. The absurdity of its opposite is demonstrated by a little-noticed incident of ten years later.[35] When C. Marius, waiting for the Germans in Gaul, found time heavy on his legions' hands, he made them dig a canal from the Rhone (above the Delta) to the sea, bypassing the mouths that were always silting up. Having dug this gold-mine, worth a fortune even in tolls and dues, he presented it, on his departure, to the loyal allied city of Massilia. (Naturally, the Massiliots proceeded to make the most of it.) This was the action of the great *Popularis*, the trusted champion of the Equites, just before 100 B.C. It is a fit comment on Roman economic interests in Gaul, then or earlier. By this time, however, failure to annex and govern had had its usual consequences: when the Germans came down on Gaul, there was no Roman governor there to meet them or to impress the restive Gallic tribes with Roman strength. We all know the result. After Marius' victories a province had to be established.[36]

The inevitable conclusion of all these considerations is that there is no evidence for an expansionist policy even after the Gracchi, if we think in terms of annexation. And we can already see that this does not fail to take account of the newly-formed (or at least newly-aroused) 'Equestrian' order, and of the very Plebs under its demagogic leaders—not to mention the Senate oligarchy which, most of the time, still governed the state according to its old-established ideas.

This conclusion is borne out by the event for which, of all events in the late second century, we have the best evidence—the Jugurthine War. In an old (but still valuable) paper,[37] De Sanctis showed that Sallust's account is utterly unreliable in its imputations of incompetence and venality to the governing oligarchy. The fact is that Numidia was being treated according to the traditional canons applied to client states that were troubled by internal disorder: with advice and *auctoritas*—including both that of personal *patroni* and that of the Senate as a whole, as weightily expressed in the embassy led by its *princeps* M. Aemilius Scaurus—but with no thought of armed intervention. Rome was accustomed to loyal obedience, and not least from the royal house of Numidia under Masinissa and Micipsa. Moreover, there was, for a long time, every reason to trust Jugurtha more than most barbarian kings: after all, he had fought at Numantia, under Scipio Aemilianus,[38] and had there met many young men who, by this time, were middle-aged men of considerable importance and influence in the state.[39] What Sallust describes as venality was, in the main, merely the natural unwillingness to think ill of an old friend, who owed his very position to Scipio's personal commendation[40] and whom it would have been rank disloyalty to suspect or to ill-treat without very good reason. We may call this gullibility; it is at least a vice common to oligarchies, to which parallels are easy to find in more recent affairs—and one due to what is basically an amiable human trait.

It is hardly necessary, nowadays, to re-argue the case for the Senate's policy in Numidia in greater detail. But if the oligarchy is acquitted of positive crime and malice, there is a temptation to put another villain in its place. For De Sanctis the answer was clear: the war was wanted by the Equites,[41] who profited by war and hoped to profit by its results. It was their aggressive interventionism that—more even than Jugurtha's own actions—helped to precipitate a costly war. Persuasively as he argues the case, we can hardly accept it as it stands. We have already seen good reason to believe that the Equites—to judge by the actions of their champion Marius, who retained their support—did not, at any rate, clamour for annexation. After all, opportunities for banking (their chief source of income) did not depend on it—as the very situation we are discussing shows: for in Numidia there was a massive Italian colony at Cirta.[42] There will be more to say about this. But it is difficult to see that the unpredictable hazards of war would have been more welcome to traders and bankers than the security of peace; or that, after a war was won, their situation was likely to be in any way improved.

Similarly the Plebs: though, aroused by its tribunes, it was only too willing—after the events of the past twenty years—to believe the worst of the oligarchs, and though it undoubtedly demanded a vigorous policy, to restore the honour of the Roman name, there is no sign of any demand for conquest or annexation, or of delight in war as such. That this was not the point is shown by the fact that all pressure ceased when Marius took over; as for the Equites, it was only the murder of the Italians in Cirta (at least some of whom will have been Romans, and all connected with Roman families) that produced a marked effect. There was an outraged clamour—and again there was every reason to believe the worst, in the light of the developing differences between the two orders that prompted Varro's famous saying that C. Gracchus had made the state 'two-headed'.[43] The Senate's failure was naturally exploited to the disadvantage of some hated figures. This explains the Mamilian commission.[44] But again, there is no reason to think that, apart from revenge, more was wanted than a serious effort to restore Roman honour and that secure peace that is always in the interests of trade and finance. What Marius promised, in his intrigues against Metellus, was a quick end to the war. As for annexation, it was never even contemplated. Not only was Marius personally entirely indifferent to it, as he was to economic exploitation—this his record in Gaul was to show; not only did he not mention either of these prizes in his propaganda before his election (which, even if we cannot accept Sallust's actual words, is probably well mirrored in the speech that Sallust assigns to him after);[45] but he did not in fact annex an acre of Numidian soil after his victory.

The final settlement was entirely on traditional lines, dividing the country between an obscure Numidian (perhaps the only member of the royal family available) who got the eastern half, and Bocchus of Mauretania, who got the western half, which Jugurtha had already promised him when he was still his ally.[46] Basically, it was the same settlement that a Senate commission had imposed between Jugurtha and Adherbal, and that Sallust, on that occasion, had viciously and unjustly attacked as corrupt and dishonourable.[47] The only real difference was that Bocchus, unlike Jugurtha on that earlier occasion, already possessed a large kingdom of his own, which he now retained in addition to half of Numidia. He thus became far more powerful than the proposed settlement on that earlier occasion would have made Jugurtha—to whose bribes Sallust claims it was due. But then (we may remember) even the Scipios had been able to boast that it was Roman practice to make friends of small chieftains and make them into powerful kings.[48] We could hardly ask for plainer proof that nothing had changed. Nor (as we have seen) did Marius, after making this settlement that did not seem to confer any advantage on any class at Rome, and that did not add an inch to Roman territory, lose the support and the confidence of Equites and Plebs —quite the opposite: he was elected, in his absence, to another consulship, which implied the command against the Germans and Gauls. As we also saw, he was to repeat his policy with regard to peace settlements in Gaul—and, after this, receive a sixth consulship, without (to say the least) any recorded opposition from disappointed supporters.[49] He had clearly done precisely what everyone wanted. At the same time, a long line of aristocratic statesmen could look down with approval on this new man permeated with their spirit, who wanted nothing more than to be like them.

THE SENATE AGAINST EXPANSION

NEITHER in the Jugurthine War, with all the bitter party politics that it called forth, nor in the German Wars at the end of the second century, was the traditional policy of avoiding major aggressive wars and administrative commitments abandoned: Numidia, where war had become inevitable, was not annexed after it; and Transalpine Gaul was at last made into a province (we do not know precisely when and by whom) for the old reason that non-annexation had turned out unsatisfactory and even dangerous: two or three garrisons, plus the services that Massilia could render, were insufficient for the proper protection of the invasion route into Italy. Indeed, not only had the traditional policies continued unchanged: it looked as if the new elements in politics—the Plebs and the Equites—which under the leadership of demagogues seemed to be challenging the oligarchy in the running of the state merely wanted a *firmer* policy (and, in its absence, were ready to suspect the worst), but had no desire to embark on a policy of aggressive war and territorial expansion. The continued loyalty they showed to Marius, who did not promise or perform anything of that sort, suffices to prove it.

That the Senate was still firmly in control on major issues was soon conclusively demonstrated by the case of Cyrene, to which we have already alluded. This kingdom, after a fashion that had begun in the middle of the previous century, was left to Rome by its last king, Ptolemy Apion, when he died in 96. Now, it is far from clear precisely what the Romans did with it, although the complex evidence has been carefully sifted.[1] But what is certain is that the Senate did not proclaim the annexation of the territory and made no attempt to take over administrative responsibility. In fact, in the unfortunate country the next two decades are mostly a period of anarchy, during which—strange as, in the circumstances of the bequest, this must seem to us—there is barely a record of any appeal to Rome, and certainly none of serious Roman interest. All that the Senate appears to have done was to arrange for the collection of some of the profits. Even this was not properly organised: no regular system was installed; there is no reference to *publicani* during the next two decades or more. When the Romans wanted to import silphium—a valuable drug, of which Cyrene was the main supplier—they seem to have paid for it (if we are to take Pliny's words at their face value).[2] We can see, not only the remarkable degree to which the Senate retained control of policy, but the absence of any major pressure in the important field of foreign policy and imperial revenues—at a time when political struggles in the city were at their fiercest and (on occasion) their most violent. The People and the Equites clearly made no attempt to force the Senate into expanding the sources of their profits, even where this could be done as easily as it in fact had been done in the days of Tiberius Gracchus. We shall see that the administration of Cyrene was properly taken in hand only in 75/4—and even then (it is legitimate to think) only in a temporary form. Indeed, it is this that gives us a clue as to what the Senate had originally intended to do about the bequest of Attalus:[3] the similarity between the two situations was so striking that, even in a society less bound by tradition, the parallel would impose itself. To the historian, this is one of the most interesting aspects of the strange affair of Cyrene.

Cyrene in 96 was a wealthy, profitable and—under a Ptolemy —a well-organised country, where annexation would have been both lucrative and easy; yet it was allowed to slip into anarchy in preference; and, in a period of bitter political controversy in Rome, not a voice was raised in protest. This is a clear example of Roman attitudes towards expansion and exploitation at this time, and indeed an outstanding one. But it is not the only one. We can see Senate policy at work elsewhere, along its traditional lines and (on the whole) equally unchallenged.

In Egypt a series of rather strange events—to which we shall return in a different connection—led to another royal testament of the type we now know so well: Ptolemy Alexander I, in 88, followed several precedents in leaving his country to Rome.[4] It was surely the richest bequest ever received, far surpassing even that of Attalus III. The Senate (under the *Populares* Cinna and Carbo) did not bother to take up the *hereditas*, merely taking care to collect a large debt owed to Romans. Nor, when things changed in Rome, did the victorious Sulla reverse that strange lack of interest in the rich prize that had so unexpectedly fallen to Rome. Far from it: he in fact sent Ptolemy Alexander II, with his blessing, to claim the kingdom. And though this Ptolemy was almost at once murdered, and this surely must have shown anyone who would look that the Ptolemies were no longer able to hold their kingdom and that annexation could hardly be escaped (not to mention the affront to Roman *auctoritas* that was implied in the murder of a king installed by Sulla)—though, moreover, only dubious claimants to the vacant throne remained—yet, despite all this, it was not until the sixties that we can see any serious pressure in Rome to claim the estate of Ptolemy Alexander I. And even this pressure, for various reasons that do not concern us yet, in the end came to nothing.[5]

Egypt, despite scrappy evidence, is a striking case. Asia is better attested. The Senate's care for the provincials of Asia is demonstrated, as late as the nineties, by the mission of Q. Mucius Scaevola Pontifex, to reform the suffering province: not that we need think this care inspired entirely by moral principles, since the constant irritation and unrest presented obvious political dangers.[6] But we must remember the original *lex repetundarum*, and bear in mind that at this time the Senate had not yet been 'reformed' by Sulla. In any case, whatever the motives, the policy is clear. Another aspect emerges, again according to pattern, in the case of Cappadocia and Paphlagonia.[7] They had been trouble-spots for years. Mithridates of Pontus, with Nicomedes of Bithynia, had invaded Paphlagonia about 104; they had partitioned it and for some time held it in defiance of the Senate's orders. As so often, the Senate, for a long time, seemed not to care. Cappadocia, which also lacked a lawful king, was the next object of their intrigues: it was no doubt in preparation for his attack on it that Mithridates was there when he met Marius. Marius visited Cappadocia in 99, when he preferred to leave the city (it was said) rather than see the triumphant return of his enemy Q. Metellus Numidicus.[8] It was also said—later—that he was looking for a chance of a military command for himself. His words and deeds belie the *ex post facto* rumour. For when he met Mithridates in Cappadocia, he gave him the famous warning: either to be stronger than Rome or to do her bidding.[9] It can hardly have been unexpected when Mithridates, on consideration, chose the more peaceful alternative. Whatever his immediate plans had been, it was clear that he could not face an ultimatum so plainly delivered. The words had been those of a man who preferred peace (with honour for Rome) to an unnecessary war; and it was probably as a result of this patriotic and successful firmness that Marius' enemies in Rome agreed to the signal honour of his augurate in absence—an unexpected honour, difficult to explain without this, but one that enabled Marius to return to Rome with his *dignitas* safe and that led to a general compromise in his struggle with his enemies.

However, the Senate still failed to act decisively in Cappadocia: Marius' brave words were not followed up in a convincing fashion. Nor was anything done to enforce belated obedience to the Senate's command in Paphlagonia. As a result of this, Mithridates proceeded to seize Cappadocia through a puppet king; and Nicomedes, worried at this, sent an embassy to Rome, which Mithridates countered with one of his own. This time the Senate made its purpose clear: the answer was that the kings must evacuate both Cappadocia and Paphlagonia. It was a stern command, which was brought to Asia by a weighty embassy headed—as an equally difficult embassy to Numidia had been sixteen years earlier—by the *princeps Senatus* himself, the (now) aged and infirm M. Aemilius Scaurus.[10] The outcome of all this, and its importance in the history of Rome at this time, I have discussed elsewhere. What concerns us here is the obvious fact that even now no attempt was made to seize the vacant territories. In fact, they were declared 'free', and the Cappadocians, disliking this dangerous and unaccustomed state, ultimately chose a king (Ariobarzanes), whom a Roman commander had to go to much trouble to instal for them. Throughout this whole affair, Senate policy is precisely what it had been in the same area in the second century: to prevent any dangerous accumulation of power—it was becoming clear that Mithridates would have to be carefully watched—but to do so with a minimum of commitment. Even Sulla, when he installed Ariobarzanes in his kingdom, seems to have had only allies and no Roman forces with him.

Now that we have incidentally come upon him, we may properly conclude this part of our survey with L. Sulla. He, of course, is the type and symbol of both the old and the new in the Roman Republic. For the moment, let us note that he firmly set his face against any expansion. His treaty with Mithridates[11]—an alliance of two dynasts against the government of Rome—cannot properly be cited in support, since at the time he was not in a position to dictate terms. But when he was already securely in power, he restrained L. Murena from harassing Mithridates and summoned him back to Rome, compensating him with a totally undeserved triumph.[12] Moreover, we have seen Sulla's action in Egypt, when he could have won ready popularity by simply accepting the bequest made some years earlier and claiming that he had added Egypt to the possessions of the Roman People—a claim that was left for another dynast to make, many years later.[13] We may also invoke the whole of Sulla's settlement of the Republican magistracies. By raising the number of praetors to eight and that of quaestors to twenty he precisely provided—as Mommsen saw[14]—for the administrative needs of the existing ten provinces, on the basis of normally annual succession. The implication is clear: he did not conceive, at least for the near future, of the annexation of any more provinces. His actions in the cases of Egypt and of

33

Murena were not isolated incidents, but part of his general scheme for Rome as he meant to establish it.

Sulla rejected the easy chance of claiming glory for the annexation of Egypt—a major acquisition if ever there was one. It is interesting, next, to note that he nevertheless conspicuously chose to arrogate to himself the glory of having extended the bounds of empire. He had, of course, celebrated a magnificent triumph—not to mention the vicarious glory of those of Murena and young Pompey[15]—to surround his usurpation with the aura of glory that, by impressing the populace, might help to erase his past and dazzle the eyes of those who disliked the armed present. But he went even further. From the annals of the distant past, he seems to have revived a long-forgotten ritual: he advanced the *pomoerium* of the city—a solemn and laborious rite, difficult enough of execution to account for the total neglect into which it had fallen for centuries.[16] This (we are told) only a man who had advanced the boundaries of Roman territory was entitled to do—in fact, strictly one who had done so *in Italy*: there could be legitimate doubt, since the ceremony had not been performed since Roman expansion beyond Italy began. Sulla (we must suspect with Mommsen) arrogated this right to himself by a trick in the best tradition of Roman legal dodges. Though he had not conquered an acre of new territory anywhere (that we know of), he extended the boundaries of Italy, for administrative purposes, from the Aesis to the Rubico[17]—not a necessary or inescapable reform in itself: the Rubico (as historians know to their cost) was not a conspicuous landmark. It is difficult to find any good reason for this action except in support of his *pomoerium* ceremony—and difficult to find any legal basis for the latter except the unnecessary reform.

We can be sure that Sulla aimed at no conquest, nor foresaw any in the immediate future. It is interesting (if the interpretation here suggested is right) that, among many actions he took for the underpinning of his detested régime by display and glory, there was a claim that was to make it appear that he *had* achieved conquest. He must have been aware that the traditional policy that he represented and reinforced was no longer one calculated to win active popularity—and that its opposite, or an appearance of it, might now do so.

Since we have anticipated to this extent, let us anticipate a little further: we are not bound to annalistic tradition. History is a series of strands, increasing from beginnings as thin as fine hairs to form stout cords, inextricably interwoven so that beginnings and ends are concealed. Sometimes a section at a given time will clarify relationships hitherto unsuspected; at other times it is best to follow individual strands before turning to the weave as a whole.

The Senate government that Sulla restored inevitably followed the general lines of the same tradition. There were indeed extensions of territory: in Isauria the conquests of P. Servilius Vatia laid the foundations of the proper territorial province of Cilicia, as distinct from the old *prouincia*.[18] But this was not a case of annexation for profit. Those hardy mountaineers, whom it took Servilius at least three years to subdue, were surely going to cost more to police and keep in order than they were likely to produce in revenue. The conquest fulfilled the demand—which had turned out to be inescapable—for a secure hinterland to the precarious coastal strip of Cilicia and for proper protection of the allied cities in the area. Seen from another point of view, again, the Isaurian war is not all that different from many other limited wars against barbarian tribes, mostly fought further west: in this case, at least, a genuine strategic need was happily combined with a commander's wish for a triumph.

Then, again, there was Cyrene.[19] In 75/4 the quaestor (or ex-quaestor) P. Cornelius Lentulus Marcellinus was sent there (*pro praetore*, it seems, though Sallust does not actually say so), to end the anarchy that had been allowed to prevail there for twenty years. This was done at the instance of some politician—perhaps (it has recently been suggested) the consul C. Cotta, whom Sallust did not like. But it is difficult not to connect L. Lucullus with the move, as consul designate in 75 and consul in 74—the man who, as proquaestor under Sulla, had called in at Cyrene, seen the condition of the country and done what, in his limited time, he could do to settle some of its problems and disputes. In any case, in 75/4 someone with *imperium* was at last specially sent there.

It must be noted that 75 was a year of famine and financial stringency—so much so that the consul C. Cotta had to make a tearful and apologetic speech to the People (which Sallust parodies with great relish) and the praetorian candidate Q. Metellus was almost lynched by a hungry mob.[20] Nothing could be done to end the famine until, in 73, funds at last appear to be available. A law of the two consuls of that year (the *lex Terentia Cassia*) provided for the purchase of extra grain in Sicily (at a fair price) and for its distribution to the People, at the rate of five *modii* per man.[21] We may wonder at the sudden affluence, at a time when a major war against Mithridates in the East had just begun, Sertorius in Spain was not yet defeated, and M. Antonius 'Creticus' was being very unsuccessful against the over-powerful pirates: in fact, in every way there were far more commitments than there had been in 75, when C. Cotta had offered up his body in expiation for the inevitable famine to the enraged crowd. The answer, of course, is easy, once the right question is asked: the money from Cyrene had come in. The People's right to profit by empire—established, as we shall see, by Tiberius and Gaius Gracchus—was beginning to break through the traditions of foreign policy. The Senate had to accept and even to encourage the organisation of a province for immediate profit. The precedent was to be remembered.

Nevertheless, it was still a very hesitant step. The Sullan Senate, clearly, was unwilling to send a senior magistrate to undertake proper administration. A junior magistrate was chosen, with the barest minimum of power.[22] He could not be a danger to the state or commit it to unwanted trouble. Moreover, it is not by any means certain that there was henceforth a permanent administration, with governors regularly sent out.[23] In 67, another (a Gnaeus) Lentulus Marcellinus is found at Cyrene as a legate of Pompey; and in that capacity he performs some of the functions

36

that, had there been a governor, were properly the governor's. He even seems to supply a date for counting years! The easiest conclusion is that there was no governor, and that P. Lentulus Marcellinus (the quaestor) had been sent, not as the first of a series of regular governors, but on a special mission for a particular purpose. What the purpose was, we have already seen: he was to reorganise the finances of the province and restore peaceful conditions, so that the Romans would at last derive a worth-while revenue from the royal estates there, which they had been exploiting ever since the will of 96, but (it seems) haphazardly and ineffectually. A large sum of money was urgently needed to relieve the dangerous famine, and P. Lentulus' main task was to find it. The choice of a quaestor was appropriate enough. Yet, however alarming the precedent, Cyrene was (of course) not an example of annexation. Quite the opposite: it provides another example of how, even at this late date, commitments were cut to a bare (indeed, an unsatisfactory) minimum—of how responsibility that was morally Rome's was avoided, rather than of a greedy or officious search for new responsibility.

Let us finally consider L. Lucullus, who (as we have had reason to suppose) was connected with the Cyrene affair. If the supposition is correct, his ideas are clear even before he went out to Asia Minor. But let us look more closely at this man whom Ferrero considered the founder of real expansionism in Rome and the creator of a new era in policy[24]—the greatest of Roman conquerors (at any rate before Pompey), who stormed through Asia Minor, first crossed the Euphrates, invaded Armenia and sacked its capital Tigranocerta. He had shown at home that he was ready to use untraditional and unsavoury methods for the sake of gaining a major command: he had intrigued with the mistress of an influential wire-puller, his own enemy P. Cethegus, in order to achieve this. In the field he was equally ready to ignore tradition: when battle was to be joined on an unlucky day (*dies ater*: it was October 6th, 69, the anniversary of the battle of Arausio in 105) and his officers drew his attention to this, he replied: 'But I shall make it a *lucky* day for Rome.' And he went on to win the most brilliant victory in the annals of the Rcman Republic: 'the sun never saw another like it.'[25] The shades of P. Claudius Pulcher and of C. Flaminius could not have been more ostentatiously defied.

Lucullus advanced as far as Gordyene, intending (it was said) to march against the Parthians; and he was stopped only by the mutiny of his men. Personal hostility and the obvious parallel of the story of Alexander the Great have done their worst: there is no good reason for believing the unfulfilled intention.[26] But the charge itself is significant. Lucullus was accused of overweening ambition: he was charged with ruling like an absolute monarch over Cilicia, Asia, Bithynia, Paphlagonia, Galatia, Pontus, Armenia and all the lands up to the river Phasis; of trying to extend his proconsular command and piling war upon war to this end. However exaggerated, these charges contain a modicum of truth; we have already seen that L. Lucullus, the relative (by marriage) of L. Sulla and the only one of his officers who, in 88, had remained loyal to the rebel marching on Rome,[27] was not a conservative noble, but a man remarkably free from traditional restraints. He was an example of the kind of ambition that was undermining the Republic. Witness the fact that, deposed from his *prouincia* by Senate and People, he yet clung to his command and would even have liked to invade Cappadocia, until his men refused to follow him: a story that, this time, we may well believe:[28] it was a matter of making good his own failure, and the point is not laboured against him in the source.

Yet what were his actual arrangements? Of course, they never reached final form, and Pompey later deliberately reversed some of them; so that our information on them is not as good as we should like. But we can see, in outline, what he meant to do. First of all, we note that he asked for the traditional commission of ten senators and was going to put his plans before them in the traditional way. (In fact, they were there when Pompey took over.)[29] He certainly meant to annex Pontus. This, of course, was now necessary on traditional grounds: it had been left free once before after defeat and had shown that it could not be trusted. We have had occasion to observe that, in such a case, the pattern of *mos maiorum* demanded annexation. But Lucullus seems not to have gone beyond this in any way. Machares, son of Mithridates, was recognised as king in the rest of his father's dominions, in the Crimea and round the north and east of the Black Sea. Later, after the conquest of Armenia, its vassals in Commagene and Gordyene were also recognised. When Lucullus crossed the Euphrates at the strategic site of Tomisa, far from putting a garrison into that important fortress long occupied by the Armenians, he presented it to Ariobarzanes of Cappadocia—who could hardly even be trusted, on an objective assessment, to hold it securely for himself once he had it. Most astonishing of all: Syria and Phoenicia, from which Tigranes of Armenia had expelled the miserable *epigoni* of the Seleucids, at least fourteen and perhaps eighteen years earlier, were returned to Antiochus XIII of that dynasty—again a man most unlikely to be able to defend his property, and one who had never in fact been master of those regions.[30]

Lucullus' personal ambition is by no means a negligible phenomenon. Yet it is clear that, as far as foreign policy is concerned, he still stood firmly in the senatorial tradition of minimising administrative responsibility. He set out to win glory and wealth for himself and (as he might argue) for the Roman People. But he did not aim to annex territory, except that of Pontus, which *mos maiorum* required him to. Nor, to his cost, did he aim to exploit provincials.

It is tempting to look for the persistence of this attitude right down to the end: the long opposition to the ratification of Pompey's *acta* after his return from the East;[31] the objections to M. Crassus' Parthian War;[32] Cato's proposal that Caesar, after his Gallic victories, should be handed over to the enemy for perjury.[33] Perhaps the genuine remains of an old attitude of restraint enter into these. There is reason to think, even at this late time, that the best traditions of the oligarchy were to some extent surviving, among men now often powerless to influence events. But one cannot insist: considerations of principle were by now far too much interwoven with internal politics and personal antagonisms.

We have had to abandon chronological order, to show that in our field, as in others, nothing at Rome changed quickly: in all its manifestations, that which in the end added up to what we call the Roman Revolution was a slow—an almost incredibly slow—process, measured by what we are accustomed to nowadays. The most terrifying and violent upheavals—riots, seditions, murders and full-scale civil wars—were remarkably unsuccessful in causing convulsive transformations of the sort we regard as almost commonplace. Right up to the early part of the first century, the forces unleashed by the Gracchi were not so much unable as (it seems) unwilling to press for major changes in the traditional foreign policy: thus a man like Marius retained the trust and the affection of People and Equites in spite of his thoroughly traditional handling of foreign and imperial affairs. And, following events almost to the end of the Republic, we have seen that, even at times of great internal tensions, the Senate and its representatives could and did continue, on the whole, to pursue the traditional policy.

All this time, of course, the process of economic penetration of the provinces was continuing. We shall have to look at it in more detail. For the moment, let us note that it was, in the second century and for some time after, a very slow process, limited by the small number of Roman citizens of the requisite wealth and standing and by the comparatively small amount of capital available, most of which was tied up in the *publica* (taxes and army supplies) or, when withdrawn from them, invested in land to make its owner socially acceptable. As for Italians: they would be considered and protected; but they were in no position to dictate policy.

This must constantly be borne in mind when we notice that there was, at the time with which we are now dealing, no pressure on the Senate to increase economic opportunities: Egypt and

Cyrene did not become matters of public contention. There was, at most (as in Numidia), pressure to protect existing opportunities. What we do not know is how far, in the time before the Social War, senators themselves had economic interests abroad. Even Cato the Elder, it will be remembered, had been interested in trade through freedmen.[34] This sort of indirect interest must have been common, on a small scale. But it did not add up to much. The *lex Claudia* had clearly been, on the whole, successful in concentrating the interest of senators on Italian land and minimising the commitment of their wealth to the chancy business of trade or even finance. That this—fully in line with responsible senatorial thinking—had been its purpose is, of course, clear from the fact that no effort was ever made to repeal it;[35] and its success is shown by the scandal that Cato seems to have caused—and by the very foreign policies that we have been considering. No ruling class whose interests were intimately bound up with overseas investment has ever behaved as the Senate did during the time we have been considering. There had always, of course, been some exploitation of provincials by governors and their staffs. As early as 171 we have evidence of it, and of the Senate's unwillingness to punish it.[36] But, as we saw, the prelude to further expansion in the 140s was a law intended to deal with this (the *lex Calpurnia repetundarum*); and when this failed to be fully effective in due course, it was—as we shall see—superseded by the legislation of C. Gracchus, which distinctly improved matters.[37] But this, in any case, was on the whole the limit of senatorial profits from the provinces.

It is only at the very end of the century that we perhaps begin to glimpse major overseas interests on the part of senators—not that we can be at all sure even then. M. Scaurus, the *princeps Senatus*, clearly kept up a profitable connection with the Equites, despite his position as head of the Senate and of the house of the Metelli. We remember how he was made one of the chairmen of the Mamilian commission, with its *Gracchani iudices*.[38] He, in a famous but desperately difficult phrase, was charged, probably at his trial for extortion, with being *rapinarum prouincialium sinus*.[39] We are left to guess how the *rapinae* actually reached his pocket: however, he was prosecuted *repetundarum* in 92, and we may surmise that he at most got his share of the plunder others had taken during provincial commands, or was too lavishly entertained when he travelled through Asia. There is no real sign of provincial investment.

Marius is more important. We cannot really prove his provincial interests either; but his connection with the Equites is obvious and need not be argued again at length; in particular, it is notewothy that he joined them in 92 in the prosecution of P. Rutilius Rufus.[40] The political situation of the moment, and old *inimicitiae*, can account for this: P. Rutilius was a hanger-on of the Metelli who had remained loyal to them, and whom Marius had no doubt learnt to hate even in Numidia.[41] But it is at least possible that Marius' own economic interests, as well as his political ones, were involved in the case, together with those of the Equites.

There must always have been some investment overseas by senators. But we have no reason to doubt that it was small, mostly indirect, and marginal in its effects. This much the facts of policy force us to conclude. For these men had the world at their mercy, and, even at their best, they were not superhuman in their code of conduct. Scaurus' *rapinae* may be of the old-fashioned sort (whether or not he was guilty). Marius, closely linked with the Equites throughout his political career, may well have shared their financial interests. But then, Marius is a new type of consular, unusual in his age; and even he shows no initiative in foreign policy. His only contribution to the exploitation of overseas lands seems to be the settlement of his veterans in Numidia; and, as we shall see, it is very doubtful whether that was his own idea.

To sum up the conclusions we have reached: senatorial capital —which, by and large, far surpassed equestrian—was not available on a large scale for overseas investment before the Social War: equestrian was, on the whole, fully committed and needed no large-scale expansion—in fact, could probably not have coped with one; the Italians were not yet able to exercise political pressure; and the Plebs, while it certainly welcomed increased benefits, had no leaders to demand them. Hence the cases of Cyrene and Egypt; and, due to Roman conservatism, the later traces of the same attitude in foreign policy. Sulla's, as so often, is the really interesting case: pretending, with hallowed and antiquarian ritual, to have achieved conquests, when in fact he had avoided them. It is the first real sign that new forces were beginning to stir.

NEW INTERESTS AND NEW ATTITUDES

FOR, naturally, there was a new breath in Roman politics, by the end of the second century B.C. The new interests that had now been given leadership were bound to make themselves felt in due course. Led by dissident and ambitious members of the oligarchy itself, who were pursuing their own purposes, the non-political classes were bound to become aware of their own importance in the game of politics and hence, where their own interests were concerned, to challenge the oligarchy and to extort consessions in foreign policy as well as in domestic affairs. The astonishing fact is that Roman conservatism which caused the changes to come about as slowly as they did and which, right up to the end, prevented a real breach over foreign policy between the governing class and the governed.

As in other spheres, it was the Gracchi who had been the originators, setting in motion forces that were ultimately able to overturn established practices. We have noted Ti. Gracchus' use of Attalus' bequest for popular domestic purposes.[1] It was the first time that the Plebs had had a major taste of the benefits of empire. Hitherto there had been distributions after a triumph, and the provinces of the Roman People had been laid under contribution for the purpose of pre-election generosity by aristocratic candidates. But these were isolated occurrences that did not add up to much. Attalus had made the Roman People *heres*, and this time there was a leader who saw to it that it reaped the full benefits. As conservatives feared at the time, the precedent was bound to have far-reaching effects. Hitherto the benefits of empire—and they were not large, if we exclude, as we must, the immediate benefits of military victory—had gone to the ruling class and those it chose to associate with it. As Ti. Gracchus is said (by his brother) to have put it: those who had fought to win them had not even a roof over their heads.[2] This is what he set out to change.

C. Gracchus himself started from this point: it was this same idea that, with the greater clarity and logic that distinguishes him, he carried a good deal further. To what extent he was following in his brother's footsteps, carrying out his announced intentions, we shall never know. Tiberius, to us, is a dim figure, seen through the distorting mirrors of his enemies' propaganda on the one hand and his brother's on the other. His plans and motives are hardly worth investigating. But what Gaius did was certainly following up the implications of Tiberius' action in assuring the full benefit of Attalus' bequest to the Plebs. Going several steps further, he applied the principle on a large scale. He undertook nothing less than to rationalise the system of provincial administration (a task which, of course, he did not live to complete) and to convert the profits to the benefit of the People of Rome as a whole, as far as, in the conditions of his time, this could be done. His reforms have been discussed often enough, and this is not the place for a list or a general discussion. Nor are we here concerned with the question of factional or 'party' interests. I will merely repeat the warning I have often expressed: that no major political action can find one exclusive explanation, and that different ways of approach are always legitimate and, in fact, necessary. In particular, politicians inevitably act with an eye to political profit; and this aim must neither be ignored and denied nor occupy us to the exclusion of anything else. My comments on C. Gracchus in this present context are (I hope) valid and important; they do not claim to be an exclusive explanation—indeed, I have myself elsewhere had occasion to stress other facets—and should not be criticised for not being what they do not set out to be. In any case, our investigation will show a careful—and, in its context, surely intended—interconnection in the major reforms undertaken by that remarkable man.

Cicero charges C. Gracchus with having pretended to care for the Treasury, while in fact draining it dry. The charge, often repeated in our sources, is based on contemporary charges: compare the anecdote of the honest L. Piso, who queued up to collect his share of the cheap grain, the distribution of which he had strongly opposed.[3] Modern scholars sometimes deny that the law of C. Gracchus involved a subsidy—thereby demonstrating the arrogance that is the besetting sin of a certain type of approach to the sources. The evidence is conclusive: in particular, we have Cicero, who contrasts C. Gracchus' *magna largitio* with the *modica* of M. Octavius' law.[4] Since he must have had the evidence for this statement, while we—with the best will in the world—know practically nothing about the day-to-day price of wheat in Rome at this time, an argument that rejects the former by starting from the latter must be dismissed as nonsense. This has had to be stated at length, since it is important to recognise that the grain law did in fact involve a *magna largitio*—i.e. a considerable subsidy from public funds. But this was not all. C. Gracchus also, for the first time, distributed provincial land to the Roman and Italian poor.[5] In view of what we have seen of the Senate's care for the interests of provincials—a care that was genuine enough within its limits, it seems, even though it would balk at sacrificing a senator to them —we can understand that chagrin at the popularity that this measure would gain for Gaius will have been reinforced, among thoughtful senators, by uneasiness at the precedent set: at the frank claim that empire was for the benefit of the ruling people. The consequences—foreseeable consequences—of further application of Gaius' logic might horrify any honest man. We have commented in passing on the fierce resistance by the Senate majority to the proposal to colonise Narbo[6]—even though there were sound strategic reasons for reinforcing that splendid site, which experienced soldiers (such as most senators were) could hardly gainsay. There were honourable men who thought that this approach to empire should not be allowed to spread.

But Gaius' ideas were not at the naïve level suggested by Diodorus: to provide a dole so as to gain a following for himself.[7] This is his enemies' proclaimed view of him, as transmitted, e.g., by Cicero. We must not be uncritical in accepting it. As I have said: one motive of a politician is always that of securing a following. But Gaius had more serious aims, which he pursued with unusual logic. As far as the Treasury was concerned, the crucial reform was that in the collection of the new Asian tribute. We have seen that, up to the middle of the century, few of the provinces had been profitable and constant warfare had been a drain on Roman resources. Down to the fall of Carthage, Sicily was probably the only province that yielded a regular surplus—perhaps it was the most profitable even for some time after, until the slave wars came and began to ruin it. But Sicily was under the *lex Hieronica*, which no honourable senator could attempt to abolish where it was, and no realistic politician would think of using elsewhere.[8]

It was the addition of Asia that made the real difference. The facts are clear, perhaps more so in the ancient sources than in most of the modern books. On its wealth and possibilities—which we need not doubt C. Gracchus could see: for he was an intelligent and educated man, and connected with Pergamum by family ties —we have the explicit testimony of Cicero, applying as late as 66, when Rome had several more provinces than she had had in 123. Even then it could be said (probably with some exaggeration, but at least without that obvious distortion that would produce what rhetors called *frigus*) that the others merely paid for themselves, while Asia was by far the most profitable of lands.[9] The provincial revenues of the Roman People at that time amounted to about 50 million denarii (see below), from (perhaps) twelve provinces; the sum—still only about 8,000 talents, to convert to the common way of calculating such large sums—was considerably more than the proceeds of half that number of provinces in 133: the annexation of Asia, in its day, must have made a positively shattering difference. Under the administration of Cicero's client L. Flaccus, a Roman was said to have paid 900,000 sesterces (= 225,000 denarii or $37\frac{1}{2}$ talents) for the taxes of Tralles alone![10] The wealth of Asia, as compared with most other provinces, explains its peculiar position in both Roman and international affairs from its coming into Roman possession right down to the end of the Republic. It is a phenomenon that deserves attention.

It cannot be pure chance that with the acquisition of this gold-mine the theory of the systematic exploitation of the provinces for the benefit of the ruling people first appears in Roman politics. It was, basically, Asia that transformed the nature both of the Roman empire and of Roman attitudes to it. We need not doubt that all this could not be foreseen in 133: though informed about the wealth of the kings of Pergamum, the Romans probably had no very accurate idea of the actual figures involved. This was one thing that the commission of five was to find out. In the end it was M' Aquillius who made the arrangements, and made them for a new province. M' Aquillius, we are informed, was one of those men whose acquittal on a charge of *repetundae* was the talk of Rome and proved to C. Gracchus the burning need for a new law on this crime.[11] In fact, the judicial aspects of his *lex* remained to plague the unhappy province until Q. Mucius Scaevola was sent out to reform it. As for finance, we cannot tell how Aquillius had arranged the taxes of Asia—perhaps (in view of the bribes he had pocketed) not for the maximum benefit of the Roman People.[12] Technically, we may take it for granted that he put the Roman People in the place of the deceased King and that—as elsewhere—the quaestor had to collect the taxes due. Now, Roman magistrates had shown that they could not be trusted, once they were out of the Senate's sight: Aquillius was one of the prime examples. It is not difficult to imagine, in view of later attested parallels, that men who extorted money from the provincials would see to it that quite a bit stuck to their hands before it reached the Treasury in Rome. In the past, with no province really a major source of profit (except for Sicily, well and safely regulated by the unique *lex Hieronica*), this had not mattered so very much, from the public point of view. There was not very much to be lost. Now matters were different. It is very likely that, whatever the faults of the settlement of Aquillius, the amounts that began to come in after he left the province and normal administration began to function (in 126, presumably, so that the first regular tribute would reach the city late in 125) proved nothing less than staggering. A man like C. Gracchus, in love with honesty and efficiency, must have thought it a major challenge: here was a chance of ridding Roman public finance of much of its happy-go-lucky procedures; of protecting the exploited provincials, while actually increasing revenue to an extent quite undreamt of, and applying to it the idea of his brother Tiberius, that such revenues should be used for the good of the People. This, and nothing less, was the aim of C. Gracchus' major reform.[13] The proceeds of the wealthiest province—so much the wealthiest that even unsatisfactory methods of collection had produced vast sums—were to be properly secured for the Treasury, and that in easily budgetable form; the provincials were to be protected from the proved rapacity of magistrates, who were to cease collecting money and to return to their proper function of judicially watching over both collectors and taxpayers; and in the exercise of this function they were to be subjected to a stringent law and made answerable to a tribunal no longer manned by their too indulgent peers. Meanwhile the Treasury, filled from this source, and assured of a regular income, could use a fair portion of it for the benefit of the People.

This is surely the basis of the Gracchan reform. Much falls into place and our admiration for this man increases. To a large extent (it must be stressed) his scheme was successful. The grain subsidy and other expenses benefiting the People did not actually exhaust the Treasury, as his enemies had claimed; the long-range budgeting made possible by *censoria locatio* no doubt helps to account for the ease with which armies were henceforth put into the field, against the Numidians and then the Germans, in spite of disaster after disaster: this time there was no sign of the serious economic strain that had been so noticeable a generation earlier. As long as Asia was safe, there was now no need for scraping and pinching. The Senate's careful attention to Asia in the nineties, which I have often tried to point out as a neglected thread in Roman politics of the period,[14] becomes easily intelligible. Moreover, the Gracchan law-courts also seem to have worked—at least for a long time. We tend to think of Rutilius; but that was thirty years later, and there are few well-meant reforms that retain their primitive glory for a whole generation. As a salutary antidote, we would do well to remember Cicero's enthusiastic praise for equestrian juries in the *Verrines*.[15] Perhaps special pleading, in part. But in fact we know that some senators were convicted, and no one (in their cases) suggests malice. To underline the strictness of the courts at their best, in this period, we have the case of C. Cato (consul 114): this man, to the amazement of later generations, was convicted of the misappropriation of the paltry sum of (probably) 8,000 sesterces (= 2,000 denarii, or $\frac{1}{3}$ talent).[16]

Of course, as we know, the system broke down in the end, owing to factors that C. Gracchus probably should not be expected to have foreseen. Like the best-laid schemes of mice and economists, it failed to anticipate future developments that, to the censorious historian, seem inevitable. It would take us too far out of our way to investigate this in detail. Suffice it to say that what happened was, above all, that the system proved a goldmine for the *publicani*, who thus came to dominate the very class that C. Gracchus had put in charge of the jury courts: a class that had always been of varied composition, and probably based on *homines municipales* and *domi nobiles*. But there is every reason to think that the trial of Rutilius was not the culmination of a long process (no source implies this), but a sudden explosion, due to an unusual situation that concentrated the worst potentialities into a horrible actuality.[17] The shock and the horror are unmistakable in our accounts: they should help to emphasise the long success of C. Gracchus' scheme, well comparable to the best of those of our own public planners.

However, what concerns us is the obvious fact that henceforth, if they but thought about it, and if certain opportunities presented themselves, both the Plebs and the most powerful section among the Equites (as we may call the new class) could hope for benefits from increasing exploitation and from further enlargement of the empire. This, for our present enquiry, is perhaps the chief effect of the reforms of the Gracchi.

Yet, as we have seen, it took a long time for the consequences to be felt. The main reason, of course, is simply Roman traditionalism: a full generation passed before it occurred to anyone that a serious challenge to the Senate on principles of foreign policy was possible. It took even longer to develop an alternative policy. We have seen that the Jugurthine War brought to a head the suspicion of the ruling class that (as Sallust saw) had long been building up and now erupted into open attacks on the *superbia nobilitatis*. But there was as yet no alternative policy—not even alternative leaders. The choice of Q. Metellus proved, for the moment, quite satisfactory and ended discontent. It was only Metellus' failure to put a speedy end to the War, and the mischance of Marius' intrigues against him, that led to Marius' election.[18] Even then, after a passing difficulty, Metellus got his triumph—no mean achievement for a man who (whatever modern scholars may have to say on who *really* won the war against Jugurtha) had obviously not finished his war and had no right to that honour.[19] It shows the hold that the oligarchy still retained. Of course, Marius was fortunate, up to a point: he *was* an alternative leader, free from the taint of nobility and with impeccable equestrian connections. Unfortunately, he had no ideas: his aim was merely to succeed. As we have seen, his settlement of Numidia is not only fully traditional, but in fact revived the Senate's earlier dispositions. The next development was due to another man, following up what C. Gracchus had begun. We have noticed how, in special circumstances, C. Gracchus' scheme for overseas settlement had been successfully revived a few years later, in the case of Narbo.[20] Twenty years after C. Gracchus, it was carried much further by L. Appuleius Saturninus.

It was Saturninus who, in 103, enabled Marius to satisfy his obligations of patronage towards his army by distributing large holdings (of 100 *iugera* each) to his veterans in Africa.[21] Unlike

C. Gracchus' colony at Carthage, these holdings—for the most part not in colonial form—survived, and their importance for the later Romanisation of Africa is well known.[22] That the idea was not the general's, but the tribune's, seems clear. For one thing, Marius had been consul in the preceding year, and had been back in Rome; yet nothing had been done for his veterans. And yet the man who had just been dispensed from the laws to hold a second consulship could almost certainly have had something done, had he known what to do. Moreover, we find Saturninus himself developing and generalising his idea in his next tribunate: as the same source tells us, he now planned for settlements of veterans in Sicily, Greece and Macedonia, as well as those in Gaul that were meant for the veterans of Marius' German War.[23] Indeed, this excessive ambition is what embroiled him with Marius and led to his downfall.[24] However, the idea itself was not forgotten: it was taken up and vigorously pursued by Sulla in Corsica, by Pompey in the East, and then by Caesar and the Emperors.[25] The settlement of soldiers on conquered land became a standard benefit that the ruling people could expect; and, at least on occasion, the poor of the city and of Italy shared in it.

It is about this time that we see the Senate, for the first time, take effective action against piracy. In 102 (as far as we can tell), the praetor M. Antonius, perhaps with consular *imperium*, was sent to a new *prouincia* of Cilicia—a *prouincia* that was not really a territorial province, but the name of a command against the pirates based on that coast.[26] It has always been recognised that this new departure—the engagement of considerable forces on this quite new task of clearing the seas—was to some extent due to pressure from equestrian circles. Moreover, M. Antonius, a man with many Arpinate connections, was one of Marius' friends and protégés. It is not fanciful to see in his selection the work of the man who, in this very year, was consul for the fourth time and who, incidentally, had in that very year helped the much-defeated Q. Catulus to a consulship that he probably no longer expected.[27] He was always the friend of the Equites.

We must add—so obvious that they tend to be overlooked—
Italian traders. We remember that many of the Italian traders in
the East come from southern Italy and many, at this time, are not
Roman citizens; but the Senate, in its role of patron of the Italian
allies, carefully watched over their interests in the provinces—
thus incidentally distracting attention from certain things that were
happening in Italy. By 100, of course, we are within a decade of
the Social War. The problem of Allied enfranchisement appeared
to have faded into the background, after the acute phase of the
120s. But that is at least to some extent due to the nature and
interests of our sources. That it was very much there still is clear
from some small facts: Marius' illegal enfranchisement of two
Camertine cohorts on the battlefield; the settlement of Italian
along with Roman veterans in Africa (to judge by the families
later found there); Saturninus' attempt to secure roundabout enfranchisement for Italians *via* the army and colonisation, and
the reaction of the Roman Plebs to this; finally the action of the
censors of 97/6, M. Antonius and L. Flaccus, in opening the
citizen lists to allies who had no right to be there.[28] This brings us
back full circle to M. Antonius: a picture of the man begins to
emerge, very different from Cicero's pious fictions. We need not
doubt that the vigorous action against piracy, at a time when
Rome could hardly afford it, was (at least in part) deliberately
taken for the sake of the Italians affected, when Italian dissatisfaction at home was becoming dangerous. M. Antonius, the
friend of Marius and of the Italians, must have his proper place in
this.

The pressure on the Senate from the new classes can be dis-
cerned; and, not unexpectedly, it is Marius and his circle whom
we find transmitting it. But, just as in the Jugurthine War, it is a
limited pressure—a pressure for the protection of existing interests,
and in general for a more vigorous policy than the Senate would
willingly have chosen: we must remember that, at this very time,
the Germans were undefeated, the slave war in Sicily was going
very badly, and there was fighting in Spain and perhaps in

Thrace.[29] There is as yet no pressure for expansion. As we have seen, it is very probable that the Equites had as much as they wanted, since their numbers were comparatively small and their capital normally fully employed. In Asia itself—where, even in the sixties, a large part of the capital of the *societates* was tied up—they were not having an altogether easy and profitable time. Only a few years later, the situation had deteriorated to an extent that made the mission of M. Scaurus and that of Q. Scaevola necessary.[30] Even earlier, the diplomatic success of Marius against Mithridates must have brought welcome relief to very sensitive investors.

In any case, however, as we shall increasingly see, good business could be done without annexation. We must remember Nicomedes III of Bithynia, who could not send Marius auxiliary forces because so many of his subjects had been taken away as slaves by Romans.[31] Despite control of the law-courts in Rome, it was perhaps more comfortable for some to be beyond the *imperium* of a Roman governor.

We have seen the limits of equestrian pressure: it was, as yet, far from alarming. The first alarming incident was of a very different nature; and it occurred in 89, while the Social War was still raging in Italy.

This time it was not a question of financiers or demagogues, of the new classes brought into prominence and made conscious of their interests by the Gracchi. It was the innate vice of the oligarchy—its inability to control its members—that was suddenly seen to be the real danger, coupled with the decline in the standards of many of those members. Even in the second century, the ambition and greed of individual nobles had sometimes set them at odds with the considered policy of the Senate. But that ambition had usually found fairly harmless outlets (harmless from the point of view of public policy) on the barbarian frontier in Liguria, Spain and other such places: many were allowed and even encouraged to indulge their ambition and their greed; others who did so against the Senate's wishes or to excess usually

54

got away with it and did no great damage to the public interest. In their dealings with major powers and civilised states, the representatives of Rome showed, on the whole, a praiseworthy sense of responsibility, and the Senate asserted sufficient control over them, so that outrageous behaviour was rare indeed and confined to conditions of special strain. Having (as we have seen) no major economic interests abroad, Roman aristocrats were less inclined to let personal factors impede their judgment. The dichotomy in Roman policy, which we noticed at the beginning, is reflected in different standards of individual behaviour and of collective control.

By 89, many factors had combined to undermine that state of affairs. Above all, Roman nobles had simply become increasingly and excessively arrogant and confident. For one thing, their heads were turned by excessive powers and excessive honours in the provinces. The Roman governor, with his permanent emergency powers, subject to no appeal and *de facto* to no enforceable law, would have had to be more than human to preserve moderation and self-restraint. And if any praetorian or consular governor became the patron and benefactor and saviour of famous cities, with statues and heroic honours to him everywhere; if the quaestor M. Annius could have games founded in his honour,[32] it was not surprising that even the civilised part of the non-Roman world gradually came to appear beneath serious notice and unworthy of Roman consideration. The consent of the governed came to matter less and less. Outside the parts directly controlled, Rome had had no major war to fight for a long time. All the wars in the East, from 200 to 126 B.C., had ended in triumph and enrichment; in the nineties of the first century, the world had seen the spectacle of the great kings of Asia Minor meekly—as usual —accepting the Senate's command, conveyed to them by the *auctoritas* of an unarmed commission. The effect can again be most typically seen in Sulla—the man whose actions so often summarise and illustrate all that one has to say about his period. When Sulla had installed Ariobarzanes in his kingdom (without meeting serious opposition) in 95, he met a Parthian embassy on the banks of the Euphrates. It was the first time that the two powers had come into diplomatic contact. Sulla ceremonially took up his seat between Ariobarzanes, the loyal and dependent client, and the Parthian envoy—thereby indicating that he regarded the Parthians in the same light as Cappadocia. (And this was well understood by the Parthian King: the envoy, on his return, was executed for submitting to it.)[33] The incident is worthy of contemplation, as showing the attitude of Roman nobles towards what remained outside the orbit of their influence. We must bear it in mind when we come to the incident of 89 B.C.

The story is most fully told by Appian.[34] Some years after Sulla's return to Rome, Mithridates had again occupied Cappadocia and had expelled Nicomedes IV from Bithynia, hoping that Rome's preoccupations nearer home would prevent her from interfering. In 89, with the Social War approaching its end, the Senate sent an embassy to restore the two kings. It was headed by M' Aquillius, son of the man who had organised Asia (and therefore one of the patrons of the whole area) and a friend and protégé of C. Marius: he had been Marius' chief legate in Gaul (103) and later his colleague as consul 101, and Marius had successfully defended him (with the help of M. Antonius) against an extortion charge a few years later.[35] It was perhaps due to Aquillius' hereditary connections that he soon succeeded in getting a force of allies together and (with the help of C. Cassius, governor of Asia) in restoring the kings. His mere presence had been enough, and there was no resistance. Mithridates, cautious as before, again preferred to pull out and wait for a better chance.

But Nicomedes, the restored King of Bithynia, had issued promissory notes for large sums to the commanders restoring him and to various eminent men in their suite: it was coming to be an expensive business to be restored to one's throne by Romans. As he had no funds for immediate payment, and his future prospects looked very uncertain (particularly in view of Mithridates' behaviour in the past), Aquillius and his friends decided that they must try to get their money as soon as they could. They black-mailed Nicomedes into plundering Pontic territory, partly per-haps (if we may give them the benefit of the doubt) in order to impress Mithridates with a show of strength, but largely to get him some funds to pay his debts. But Mithridates was not pre-pared to be insulted and intimidated: the result, before long, was the First Mithridatic War.

Appian makes out (no doubt from his source) that Aquillius positively wanted to start a war, without reference back to Rome (he insists on this), and that this was the real aim of his pressure on Nicomedes. On general grounds this might appear quite credible; but it is belied by the facts of the case as Appian himself gives them, and it may be regarded as an obvious *ex post facto* comment. When Mithridates sent an embassy to protest at the raids into his territory, the reply he received was in fact anything but pro-vocative or insulting. The Romans replied that 'they would not wish Mithridates to suffer harm at the hands of Nicomedes, but would not permit Nicomedes to be attacked by armed force'—i.e., Mithridates could not expect reparations and would not be allowed to extort them (it is this that makes the chief object of the exercise—the winning of booty—clear); but that, if he refrained from retaliating, there would be no further attacks. It looked as if Aquillius had achieved his limited objectives, and the reply quoted makes it clear that he had no intention of going further.

But Mithridates, outraged by what had happened, refused to negotiate. He felt strong enough to fight, and he now had an excellent pretext: indeed, it looks as though he was already regretting his earlier decision to pull out, perhaps in the light of more accurate information about the strength of the forces actually at Aquillius' disposal. His propaganda line could now be the one that is reproduced for us, on a later occasion, by Sallust: that the Romans were seeking to subject the whole world to their greed, that they were *latrones gentium*.[36] Having his pretext, he at once invaded—not Bithynia, which had technically been the guilty party, but Cappadocia, where he easily expelled the unfortunate and quite guiltless Ariobarzanes. At this point, of course, the Romans had no option but to fight, even though their forces were inadequate and their allies unreliable. M' Aquillius, captured by Mithridates, was killed by having molten gold poured down his throat—a public illustration of the King's official *casus belli*.

It was the first time that a major war had been brought about by an individual Roman acting on his own initiative. Yet, despite what was to be said about it later, it arose (it seems) from a miscalculation rather than from deliberate provocation: it is clear that it was ultimately Mithridates, and not Aquillius, who really wanted to fight. Unaccustomed to opposition, and treating eastern kings as helpless clients (in the light of past victories and past and present servility), Aquillius blundered into war while trying to satsify his own greed and that of his associates; though it can even be argued that he may have conceived of the raids as a (by Roman tradition) legitimate terrorising operation and that, had he succeeded, he would have earned nothing but praise in Rome. The real significance of the incident is that it was an attempt at blatant enrichment by a senator at the expense of a king who, up to that point, had loyally obeyed Rome's command—and an attempt entered into, as was to appear only too clearly, without adequate consideration of the probable consequences and without even sufficient force to back it at all plausibly. Since Aquillius was such a close associate of Marius, it has inevitably been asked whether Marius was also involved. Certainly Marius, by now, had no fear at the propect of an eastern war. Having failed to gain the distinction he wanted in the Social War, he had withdrawn from it in disgust: he now seemed eager for a special command that would at last bring him another appeal to save his country and would fulfil the seer's promise of a seventh consulship.[37] Perhaps Marius had been one of those who had lent Nicomedes money towards his restoration, or had been promised some for favouring it: with his Asian connections, he could hardly fail to be courted. In any case, it is very likely—though we cannot prove it—that he approved of Aquillius' handling of the situation and actually welcomed the war that resulted from it. The personal foreign interests of Roman senators had made an impressive entrance on the stage of history.

The Jugurthine War had already produced the suspicion that the ruling class was sacrificing the national interest to that of its individual members. It was of course true (and always had been) that great men received worthy presents from their clients abroad for the patronal services that they performed. That was *mos maiorum*, inextricably interwoven with ancient social conventions. It was only when things went wrong, and when slowly developing suspicion was stirred up by orators, that people began to suspect this traditional practice.[38] At the time (as we saw) they were wrong: there is no evidence that the presents that Jugurtha must undoubtedly have given to his Roman patrons made any difference to Roman policies. By 89 the decline in the morality of the upper class is becoming visible: the stakes were now enormous, and some felt that there was no longer any need to give careful consideration to the consequences of the pursuit of private interests in public policy. It was an early sign of the storms to come.

THE NEW IMPERIALISTS: THE MYTH

THE Social War and the civil wars that followed hastened the decline and completely changed the picture. They had a profound effect on both the moral climate and the social and political structure of the Roman Republic. Let us first look at the social and economic results.

We have noted that in the second century there does not—at least until near the end—appear to be any large-scale exploitation of the Empire. Individual members of the ruling oligarchy derive their profits, lawful and illicit. But the Senate as a whole seems sincerely concerned (though not always successful in its efforts) to stop the illicit sort; and excessive profits by citizen contractors are for a long time discouraged—as is clear from the outstanding example of the Macedonian mines.[1] On the other hand, trade and finance by Romans and by Italians flourish under official protection, in provinces and 'free' territories, particularly in the East. But again, there is no sign of serious exploitation. In the free harbour of Delos, where the Italians attain the summit of their power and prosperity, that of the Syrian colony almost equals theirs.[2] C. Gracchus, for the leading and most enterprising men of non-senatorial rank, laid the foundations of the wealth and power that would end by rivalling those of the Senate. But there were few of them; and, as we saw, their capital was probably too limited for any major expansion of investments, even had the chance offered. In fact, imperialism in its economic aspects is still very restrained, in comparison with the size of the empire and the extent of Roman power and influence.

The war that began in 91 and lasted, in some form, until about 80 had one important result, and an immediate and practical one

—one so familiar that we are in danger of overlooking its consequences: Italy received the Roman citizenship. The chief consequence was the transformation of the Roman upper class. This, of course, was what Roman upper-class opponents of this reform—men like the consul L. Marcius Philippus and those senators and equites who rallied in his support in 91—had always feared.[3] Not indeed that there was a flood of new men in the highest places: it is unlikely that anyone had seriously expected this. Syme and others have fully demonstrated the extreme slowness of this particular process, due to the restraints of the system and to the conservatism of the Roman electorate. In 63 B.C., defending L. Murena—a man of distinguished and long-standing praetorian family who had won the consulate against a *nobilis* of ancient, but not recently prominent, lineage—Cicero had to meet a strong *prima facie* presumption that such a success could be due only to corrupt practices.[4] The most interesting feature of his remarkable and instructive speech on that occasion is the fact that this argument could not be simply laughed out of court: the immense seriousness with which the orator treats it—devoting a large part of his speech to its thorough refutation—shows as nothing else can the enduring and even increasing right to high office of the old *nobilitas*. However, at lower levels—particularly where the *comitia tributa* elected—the trickle of municipal men had by mid-century become a steady stream; and most of Italy was by then represented among the back-benchers: *homines noui et parui senatores*,[5] who nevertheless could at times make their presence felt. Many of these men belonged to the municipal aristocracies of Italy and had wealth not out of place even in the Roman Senate.[6] And many of them were related to the *negotiatores* (financiers and traders) who, generations ago, had already been making their fortunes overseas. At the same time, all of them were amply endowed with Italian land. In this way new links were forged and maintained between Senate and Equites, who had been drifting apart for political reasons ever since C. Gracchus 'threw daggers into the forum' and who had reached an impasse of opposition by

90 B.C. Sulla himself, by his adlection of about 300 equites into the Senate, had made a decisive start.[7] Henceforth there is no clear boundary between the orders, in status or interests. The post-Sullan—much more than the immediate pre-Sullan—Senate is linked with the equestrian order through its lower representatives, sharing interests and interrelationships; and this was soon to appear clearly in politics: not only in the provincial interests of senators, which now take on increasing importance and more clearly defined shape (as we shall soon have occasion to see), but in the accord of 70 over the law-courts. This accord, accepted by the best men in the Senate and causing no dissatisfaction among the Equites, would have been quite inconceivable a generation earlier—indeed, when the consul Q. Servilius Caepio tried to achieve something very like it in 106 B.C., it lasted only for a short time and was much disliked.[8] Now, agreement continues undisturbed until the nature of the law-courts themselves is radically changed under the Empire. Nothing can more clearly illustrate the immense change—despite occasional differences between them—that had come over the relationship between the two orders; and it was, of course, against this background, much better known to him than it is to some moderns, that M. Tullius Cicero developed his scheme for a *concordia ordinum* to save the Republic—for which he has many times been unreasonably criticised.

But the *ordo equester* itself demands our careful scrutiny. It is odd that until quite recently it had never been properly surveyed and discussed, in spite of all the interest that modern scholarship has shown in this period. The details of how the early *equites Romani* (limited in numbers and duly enrolled by the censors—and alone entitled to certain specified privileges) were merged and submerged in the inflated *ordo equester* of Cicero's day are, in important respects, still impenetrable and, in any case, cannot be discussed here.[9] The fact is that equestrian status in Cicero's day was based on a mere qualification of wealth;[10] hence the wealthiest element was dominant, particularly the *publicani* of the big

62

societates. This, however, meant that the *ordo equester*, unlike most things at any period of Roman history, was radically transformed almost overnight by the Social War. For once, the flood-gates were open, and all municipal notables, as far as we can see, could soon claim to be *equites Romani*. The effects of this must have been considerable, and only some of them (of relevance to us) can be considered here.

The *conuentus* of Italians in the provinces (including Roman citizens) had always been in a favoured position, owing both to the presence of those Roman citizens and to the protection that the Roman state accorded to the nearest of its clients. But now they were no longer clients. They were all full members of the master race. It was these men (the *prouinciales*) who were the chief advisers of the governor, sitting on his *consilium*, providing his juries and his agents, and (in general) furnishing that necessary element of local expertise and continuity that the Roman official machinery conspicuously lacked. They, among hostile or fawning subjects, were the only men whom the governor could fully trust. As Cicero makes clear to his brother Quintus, they were also his chief temptation and worry.[11] Especially as they must on no account be offended: the governor's future—even his *caput*, i.e. his status as a full and honoured citizen—depended on them and on their Roman friends and associates, the senators and equites who sat on the juries. A false step could end a great man's career. L. Lucullus, by a fair and reasonable settlement of debts in the ruined province of Asia, incurred their dislike—and had to pay the penalty, with Senate and People uniting to divest him of his powers, despite the friends and relations he had among the noblest in the land.[12] Things had been very different in the nineties. L. Lucullus was recalled in disgrace, and it was several years before he was, almost contemptuously, allowed to triumph[13]—a blow that broke his strong and acute mind and made him end an active life in shallow self-indulgence and ultimately madness.

Speech after speech by Cicero, in prosecution and defence—the *Verrines*, the *pro Flacco*, the *pro Fonteio* and others—attests the power and the connections of these provincial Romans, many of whom, a generation ago, would at best have been clients of the great Roman families. And we can see the multiplicity of their interests, as *publicani*, *negotiatores* and large provincial landowners —all interlaced. They were all citizens now, and the richest of them *equites Romani*: the *publica* (and especially the taxes) were open to them, and they could combine them with other interests in a formidable power. The *ordo equester* as a whole, therefore, was immensely strengthened by this infusion of new blood and new capital, and (not least important) new experience of provincial business. These men could exercise power hitherto undreamt of and form ambitions hitherto inconceivable. The resources of the provinces accumulated in their hands. Their dedications to Roman magistrates survive in large numbers—from Delos, Aegium, Argos, Cos; from Agrigentum and Panormus (to take only those represented in our most accessible selection of inscriptions).[14] Their immense wealth and power are sometimes illustrated in startling flashes—all the more startling (to us in our ignorance of the basic tone of ancient life, even at well-attested periods) when, as so often happens, they arouse no interest in our sources and no comment as being out of the ordinary.

The Civil War, particularly, forced some of these interests into —often unwelcome—publicity. In the 'free city' of Utica a body of 300 seems to be a kind of governing body of the Roman *conuentus*: no doubt the wealthiest among the community, from whom the other *negotiatores* are distinguished. They chose to support the Pompeians and at one time seem to have been practically in control of the city; but they were punished by Caesar.[15] In the little town of Thysdra Italian *negotiatores aratoresque* (note the combination) had deposited 300,000 bushels of wheat.[16] In Spain, Romans (including Roman knights) of local origin or connections fight prominently on both sides: there is Q. Pompeius Niger of Italica, who is the Caesarians' champion in a famous duel that gives our pedestrian author the chance of emulating the grand historical tradition; Baebius, Flavius and Trebellius (all three *equites* from the little town of Asta) desert to Caesar, 'their horses almost covered with silver' (as the author disapprovingly notes), and report that all the Roman knights in the Pompeian army (i.e. all those recruited in the province?) had wanted to desert, but had been found out and imprisoned.[17] A Caesarian party sent to Ursao contains senators and knights, including some (knights, presumably) belonging to the city.[18] Of the 3,000 knights who fell at Munda, some were from Rome, others from the provinces.[19]

We cannot tell how many of all these and other men mentioned were veterans recently settled there, how many enfranchised natives (as—one would think—Q. Pompeius Niger was), how many settlers of Italian origin and how many actual Italian businessmen. No doubt all these classes were represented. They all now formed the ruling class of provincial society and politics, dominating the provinces of the Roman People, and in constant touch with their associates, their friends and their families at home. The *ordo equester* had absorbed Italian notables and (like the roll of citizens as a whole) had thereby become wide open, recruiting new strength from provincial sources. It is strange that the story has not been properly told. Even Rostovtzeff, who well knew how greatly the enfranchisement of Italy increased the resources of this class, was unfortunately the captive of his own theory of an overriding conflict between the proletariate and the upper class: he saw in the *ordo equester* of the Ciceronian age only a force that 'strengthened the ranks of the existing order' against proletarian revolution—a view that has an element of truth, but, like many such, is all the more misleading on account of it—and that supported the Roman government's policy of imperialism which he claims to recognise even in the second century.[20] We have already seen that this last view flies in the face of the evidence; and we must now note the havoc that it wrought—except where his profound knowledge of the facts broke the shackles of theory—in his whole interpretation.

There is a major task—or rather, several major tasks—still to be done. We cannot do it here. Let us, however, briefly glance at two provinces, representative in their diversity, for which we have rather more detailed evidence.[21]

In Asia, as is well known, Italian interests were prominent enough—and Italians sufficiently hated—for Mithridates' order for the slaughter of Italians to meet with overwhelming success. 80,000 Romans—as they now were, in law as well as in name—are said to have been killed in one day.[22] It was only in 81, after Sulla's victory and the return of settled conditions in the Roman world, that any large number of men expelled from the province can have returned. In 74 there was no massacre; but we can be certain that the old memory caused a mass exodus of Romans. It took some time to reconquer Asia and make it safe for exploitation once more. Lucullus' settlement is probably to be dated around 70. To what extent the Romans in the province had soon recovered and consolidated their power there is clear from the *pro Flacco*, dealing with the situation only a few years later. The speech is (it might seem to us) quite disproportionately full of Roman interests in Asia: three Roman knights in the province (s. 31); an estate at Cyme belonging to a Roman orphan and bought by a Greek with money he has borrowed from two Romans (apparently coming to Rome for the purpose: s. 46); property at Temnus and at Apollonis (a 'free' city) owned by Decianus, one of the prosecutors (51f. and 70f.); payment of a large debt extorted by the Roman Castricius—member of a family of *negotiatores* well known in the East—from Tralles (53f.); the interests of Lurco and Septimius (87f.). And there are two very odd incidents: Cicero's client, as governor, had (it seems) got hold of the estate of a Valeria who had died intestate—one of his actions that even his attorney can hardly justify as anything but dubious (84f.); and Falcidius, a Roman living (as is clear) in Asia, had given the governor 50 talents (= 1,200,000 HS)—or so he said—and had almost ruined himself by doing so: this man (we learn) had paid 900,000 HS for the taxes of Tralles alone (90f.)—no doubt regarding this as a sound investment. As can be seen,

66

much of the speech is taken up with the interests of Roman citizens in Asia.

But we know, in a more general way, that even by 66 the Romans had flooded back—only three or four years after the completion of the reconquest. In that year, Asia was by far the principal source of revenue for the Treasury, and most of the property of the honourable gentlemen of the tax companies was invested there; others were engaged in business there and had most of their capital actually in the province: a large number of citizens was involved in all this; moreover, as Cicero points out (as a well-known and universally accepted fact), a collapse of credit in Rome itself was the inevitable consequence of even a mere threat to Asia.[23] So much had been restored in a very few years.

Next, Transalpine Gaul.[24] As we have had occasion to notice, there is no sign of serious Roman interest there before the German wars. We can therefore all the more easily observe the speed of Roman penetration after. It was apparently the German wars that first led to the establishment of a regular province—and to penal confiscation of land. This kind of punishment seems to have been greatly extended in the province during the next few decades, as repeated revolts had to be suppressed. Around the middle 80s B.C., we get a sudden glimpse of what was going on in the province. An early speech of Cicero's (the *pro Quinctio* of 81, dealing with events of a few years earlier) turns on the exploitation, by two Romans in partnership, of a highly productive farm and ample grazing lands in Gaul. Even as early as that, this was apparently nothing at all out of the ordinary, and no word of explanation or comment is given—or felt to be needed—for this background. Around 75, the governor M. Fonteius (later another of Cicero's clients) is found evicting Gauls from land that had been confiscated—some (if not most) of it apparently by Pompey on his way to Spain.[25] Cicero, speaking in the early 60s, insists that heavy confiscations were specially characteristic of the province. By that time it was 'referta negotiatorum, plena ciuium Romanorum'. In fact, he adds, no business in the province is carried out without the intervention of a Roman citizen, no money changes hands without being recorded in a Roman ledger. But there is not only finance (always the speciality of Roman citizens). The large numbers of Romans in the province are analysed for us as consisting of the colonists at Narbo and 'publicani agricolae pecuarii ceteri negotiatores'.[26] The stress on land, of course, fully confirms what we have inferred must have been the position as early as the 80s. It is at this time that the old prohibition of vine and olive culture, which Cicero found in an early treaty,[27] must have taken on the significance that he then (as we saw) retrojected—misleadingly for the modern scholar—right back to its origin. In fact, the prohibition, as is clear from the wording quoted, does not apply to all land in the province (as is often mistakenly suggested by modern interpreters): it is limited to land in the hands of the natives (*transalpinae gentes*). It would in any case have been difficult to believe, at this time, in a provision forbidding the growing of vines and olives on land held anywhere by Roman citizens; but as it happens, there is no mention of them in the prohibition as reported—surely not through Cicero's carelessness. The old treaty had developed—accidentally, but much to the liking of many Romans—into a highly protective measure, favouring, not so much Italian land as against provincial, as the interests and the profits of the numerous Italians whom we find owning and holding land in the province at this time. The development is a measure of the change in the situation as a whole.

We have looked at two provinces. But, where we have the evidence, a similar picture can be glimpsed in others. Cicero's letters of recommendation (Book xiii of his *Letters to his Friends*) provide interesting material, despite their superficially dull uniformity. Large interests, landed and commercial, can be documented in several provinces. There is other sporadic evidence, illuminating even the most obscure corners of the Roman world. In Illyria, Salonae was probably conquered (by C. Cosconius) as late as 78 B.C., in one of the border wars that—as we saw—continued in this period as before.[28] By the time of the Civil

War, its Roman *conuentus* was a firm and important ally of Caesar.[29] The island of Issa, long a 'free' city, is found sending an embassy to call on Caesar during his proconsulate: the embassy is headed by a Gavennius, clearly a Roman citizen.[30] The Illyrian city of Lissus, in fact, appears to have been handed over to its Roman *conuentus* by Caesar at some time (we cannot tell how long) before the Dyrrhachium campaign, possibly owing to some act of disloyalty on the part of the natives.[31]

There is no doubt that imperialism, in the sense of exploitation by the ruling power, developed enormously after the enfranchisement of Italy and the consequent strengthening of the equestrian order. The rapidity of the Romans' return to Asia (followed, no doubt, by further expansion there), of their penetration of the province of Transalpina and even of little-noticed Illyricum, and the speed with which they succeeded in seizing an important and powerful position there, is particularly startling in view of the general slowness of transformations—political and economic— under ancient conditions. Nothing quite like this, probably, can be seen in antiquity, except perhaps the Greco-Macedonian penetration of the Middle East after Alexander the Great. In Roman history, certainly, the phenomenon is unusual. It will be our next question whether and to what extent this affected imperialism in the other main sense—that of actual expansion. We have seen that right up to the Social War there is no evidence of expansionist pressure by the Equites; and perhaps we have even caught a glimpse of the answer to our question about what followed. However: what difference did the enormous increase in the power and the resources of the order make to foreign policy?

It might seem obvious, from all the facts we have been investigating, taken in the context of our modern experience, that the *ordo equester* of the age of Cicero, with its greatly increased capital and its power in the law-courts, and with its almost uncannily dynamic expansion in the provinces of the Roman People, must have been constantly pressing for further increases in its opportunities by further extension of the frontiers, for more room

F

to plough back its profits and thus expand them. It might seem so obvious that one need not prove it. Thus for Tenney Frank, who knew Roman economic history better than almost anyone else has ever known it, and who was the foremost opponent of those who (like Rostovtzeff) saw an imperialist policy based on economic motives in Roman expansion in the second century—even for Tenney Frank there was no question about it: L. Lucullus' failure to annex Syria annoyed those interests in Rome; and the result was that Pompey, whom they had learnt to trust, was substituted for Lucullus, on the understanding that there would be some highly profitable annexation after all: 'Three years later (after 70) the knights had their reward when the same elements combined in a demand that Pompey clear the seas of pirates . . . and the year after commissioned him to destroy Mithridates and organize the East in a series of provinces which would be open to commercial "development".'[32] Fortunately, this thesis has not found general acceptance; but even where not accepted, it has more often been ignored—by scholars less familiar with economic history than Frank—than considered and refuted; and it is therefore, at least as a general thesis, at times fashionably revived.[33] It will thus now be worth our while (before we look at the positive content of Roman 'imperialism' towards the end of the Republic, and at its real bases) to show that the conclusion to which our argument in the preceding pages seems to have been leading with irresistible force—that it was pressure from the Equites, after the Social War, that transformed the nature of Roman imperialism and made it consciously expansionist—is in fact totally invalid; except for what we have already discussed at length, the thorough exploitation of the empire within its existing boundaries, and of territories beyond those boundaries, which we may justly describe as itself a form of imperialism.

There is surprisingly little evidence that at this time trade preceded the flag. This is surprising because in the second century we do find large colonies of Italians beyond the boundaries of the empire in its strict sense—at Delos, at Cirta, and in other places still technically 'free'. Yet in the first century, despite the far larger resources and the rapidly increasing penetration of the provinces that we have noticed, there is little evidence for such movements. In distant Noricum (it has been said)[34] Roman traders appear by the middle of the first century; but reviewers have been very hesitant to believe it, and the evidence for such infiltration during the late Republic appears rather weak. In Germany, Caesar refers to trade with the Suebi;[35] and many— including no less an authority than Sir Mortimer Wheeler[36]— have taken him to mean *Roman* traders. Yet it is surely odd that Caesar does not say so: why not 'nostri', since it was anything but self-evident? Such silence is at least suspicious. In independent Gaul (before Caesar's conquest) some Roman objects begin to spread north. But again, they appear to be few;[37] and there is no real reason to think that it was Romans who carried them—no mention, e.g., in Caesar, who could hardly have failed to come across such men.

Of course, there are the Roman *negotiatores* at Cenabum, who were massacred at the outbreak of the final revolt.[38] But by then Caesar had been fighting in Gaul for six years—long enough for the army (and its rich booty, not to mention its need of supplies) to have attracted the usual following of civilians. That this was the origin of the Romans there is suggested by the fact that among them there was killed an *eques honestus* who, by Caesar's command, was in charge of the food supply of the army. It is not difficult to deduce the nature of the main 'business' done by the Romans at Cenabum. The picture we are given of the Belgae at the beginning of the War—still almost uncorrupted by imports of luxuries from the Province—makes it clear that there had, at least, not been any very thorough and far-ranging penetration by Romans.[39]

Similarly in Syria, with which we started. Before annexation— as Rostovtzeff acknowledges, though he oddly denies that it is significant[40]—there is a remarkable dearth of Romans; yet afterwards they soon appear in large numbers. Perhaps one should not press mere arguments from silence: we cannot deny that a certain

71

amount of trade will have been carried on by Roman citizens, in Syria as in Gaul. But it is surely significant when a dearth of evidence about their doings before annexation contrasts both with abundance of it after and with the ample attestation of their presence, both in literature and in the documents, within the bounds of the empire.

We should probably accept the conclusion suggested by the evidence: that, at the time we are considering, Roman capital was, on the whole, concentrating on the thorough penetration of the existing provinces. Under the protection of the Roman name, and of magistrates who shared in these interests and whose future was in the hands of the businessmen's associates in Rome, this was very much easier and more convenient than pioneer work in remote parts—and by now, parts not under Roman control were in fact getting more and more remote. In other words: the— perhaps paradoxical—effect of the transformation and explosive growth in manpower and resources of the *ordo equester* seems to have been a turning inward, upon the empire as it was, of all the vast resources now available. That this would not have remained the case for long can easily be argued: there was to be no chance to find out. But it does seem to be true of at least a moment in time—and, of course, it makes the startling development of Roman penetration in the existing provinces, on which we have commented, very much easier to understand.

There is another point to consider. The very wealthiest of Roman *negotiatores* (at least of those in the city) were probably still in finance rather than in trade. This was the traditional form of Roman *negotia*, and we have it attested for Gaul and elsewhere. And this kind of business, far more than trade, could be very satisfactorily carried out in settled and dependent client states—as Roman senators were also to find. Kings were always clamouring to be recognised or supported against enemies, and they were chronically short of money and forced into borrowing, both to pay for these services and even to keep up with the accumulating interest they already owed. For the really large-scale financier—

72

and, as we shall see, he was more likely to be a senator than a knight—kings were profitable business. We remember how, even around 100, Nicomedes III had had masses of his subjects sold into slavery.[41] In the first century we find that a *senatus consultum* had apparently forbidden the making of loans to foreigners in Rome.[42] A. Gabinius, as tribune (67) or as consul (58), confirmed the prohibition.[43] By 58, as we shall see, it was both highly necessary and bound to be ineffective. But the effect of this regulation was that the most lucrative business was reserved for those who could obtain exemption from the law at the hands of the Senate[44] —and that their interest rates became all the higher. We shall come back to this.

But it is at this point and in this rather unexpected connection that *equites Romani* appear in high politics, and make it clear how little they cared about annexation—or needed to.

As early as 88, we find someone—and it is surely Roman financiers—lending a large sum of money to an Egyptian king (Ptolemy Alexander I) to enable him to collect a fleet and regain his throne.[45] The circumstances of the time were exceptional, since Mithridates had made investment in Asia temporarily impossible, and some people no doubt had money to spare. As a security, they got a will bequeathing Egypt to the Roman People. When Alexander failed to regain his throne and was killed in the attempt, the Senate (by then under the *Cinnani*) made sure they got the money back; but no action was taken to annex the kingdom: this, as we had occasion to notice earlier, still seemed to be too contrary to traditional policy. It was only twenty years later, in very changed conditions, that the action of reclaiming the money could be interpreted by those in favour of annexation as *pro herede gestio*[46]—even then unsuccessfully, as it turned out.

In the early fifties, a similar situation arose.[47] Some equestrian circles had lent what was probably an even larger sum (6,000 talents = 144,000,000 HS) to Ptolemy Auletes who, though he had occupied the Egyptian throne, was much concerned to secure recognition: for his legitimacy was impugned and there

73

were at that time circles in Rome—led by M. Crassus, who had represented similar interests even some years earlier—that favoured annexation, based on the old testamentary disposition. But in 59, for the large cash payment mentioned, Caesar as consul secured Ptolemy's recognition, and the old will is not heard of again. A little later, however, Ptolemy was expelled by his subjects: his large investment had bought him only a year's respite. He now began trying to get some Roman to restore him—an issue that kept politicians agitated for years. In the end, he borrowed the truly fantastic sum of 10,000 talents (= 240,000,000 HS)—600 times the 'equestrian census' and more than the total of Roman revenues from the provinces before Pompey's eastern conquests.[48] This was the sum he paid to Gabinius—and perhaps to others who backed Gabinius' action—in order to be restored and have a Roman garrison to protect him. We happen to know about this only because a man called C. Rabirius Postumus—son of an old client of Cicero's—arranged the loans and, when Ptolemy returned to Alexandria, became his minister of finance, to see that the interest was paid and the debt collected; and because both Gabinius and Rabirius were later prosecuted for their parts in the affair and defended by Cicero.[49] This incident is the best example we have of the enormous sums now at the disposal of Roman capitalists, and of the influence they could exercise on international affairs. It also satisfactorily proves that this influence was not exercised in favour of annexation and direct control. Indeed, we begin to see that there might after all, in a special case, be something to be said for being well away from the scrutiny of a Roman governor.

Nor—since this is the point with which we started—had the Equites much to do with the annexation of Syria. We have already seen that they seem to have shown little interest in that region before its annexation. The latter was entirely conditioned by political and strategic considerations of a traditional sort. For Antiochus XIII, to whom Lucullus had given the country, was almost at once captured, and a pretender called Philip, after paying

74

a heavy sum to the governor of the adjacent province of Cilicia, was at that time struggling hard to maintain himself against two Arab chieftains. Soon he too disappears from our accounts, and Antiochus briefly returns.[50] Whatever precisely was happening, it is clear that Lucullus' experiment had failed and that by the time of Pompey's arrival the Seleucids had shown themselves completely incapable of holding what they had been given: peace could no longer be guaranteed without annexation. Lucullus himself, had he stayed on, might well have had to change his mind: he would hardly have left mere disorder behind him. The local situation suffices to explain the decision: there is no need even to think that Pompey was dreaming of a Parthian War, or that the Syrian coast was a base for pirates.[51]

We do not know for certain what Pompey did with the taxes of Syria; or, for that matter, with those of Bithynia-Pontus, which he also organised as a province. We hear of *pactiones* by cities with *publicani*, in which Gabinius, as governor, interfered: within a few years the *publicani* were clearly becoming a scourge and Gabinius, at what he must have known was great risk to himself, took strong action against them, in defence of nations born to be slaves.[52] This makes it most probable (though admittedly not certain) that Pompey had extended the system that had worked so well—for the Treasury—in the case of Asia, i.e. *censoria locatio*. (This, of course, would also help to explain the numerous attempts made after that time to get censors elected.) Naturally, such a policy would also gain him friends among the richest of the Equites—not to mention senators: it is a very reasonable assumption that many senators, by now, had an interest (perhaps even an open one) in these lucrative contracts, and that M. Crassus, when he worked for remission of the Asian contract in the late sixties, had more motives than mere benevolence and justice.[53] Indeed, the enormous sums involved in the contracts would much more easily be found, if the larger fortunes of senators were also engaged—and this is surely how there could still be enough left over for Ptolemy Auletes.

THE NEW IMPERIALISTS: THE FACTS

THE imperialism (in Tenney Frank's sense) of the Equites turns out to be a myth—another example of compelling modern analogies applied without due scrutiny of the ancient background. But what about the Plebs? As we have seen, even Sulla had recognised that it was susceptible to the glory of conquest; and Pompey did not fail to celebrate a magnificent triumph and games to parade his own. Cicero's speeches[1] are full of naïve patriotic appeals. Moreover, the actual profits of empire now had to go to the Plebs as much as to the upper classes—not, of course, because of any newly-developed sympathy for it, but because of its greatly increased political importance in the struggles of the oligarchs. This power, ever since the Gracchi, had often been demonstrated to full effect. The Plebs had come to regard the economic benefits of empire, first handed over to it by the Gracchi, as its birthright. Again and again we see the ideas of the Gracchi and of Saturninus taken up, and the oligarchy has to submit, in at least some cases unwillingly. We have seen how a shortage of grain and money brought about some action on Cyrene in 75/4, after the Senate had neglected it for twenty years.[2] It was this precedent that P. Clodius remembered when, in 58, at another time of shortage, he wanted to gain support for himself by making the grain distribution an entirely free gift. This, of course, imposed an unparalleled and unbearable strain on the Treasury.[3] But Clodius calmly proceeded to provide the necessary funds by passing a law annexing Cyprus—another rich Ptolemaic possession, still recognised as 'free'. The proceeds of the royal estates alone were to come to 7,000 talents and proved welcome indeed in 56.[4]

It is easy enough to see the line that goes from Tiberius Gracchus' use of the Attalid inheritance, through the organisation of Cyrene, to the culmination of the Cyprus incident. As in the other cases, the Senate could not resist. For Clodius' law was there to stay, for obvious political reasons, and the money simply had to be found. And so the virtuous M. Cato himself went out to sell the King's property and ensure that every last penny was squeezed out and accounted for;[5] and the King committed suicide in shame and despair. The organisation of the new province was settled by the Senate: it was joined to Cilicia and received its *lex prouinciae* from P. Lentulus Spinther, first proconsul of the united province. Thus the Senate assumed full responsibility. The thinking of the majority of its members was by now no longer guided by principles of—even limited—morality: such opposition as there was, to this most disgraceful act of Roman imperialism apart from the Gallic War, was obviously based to a large extent on reasons of internal politics and personal antagonism. In 63, when P. Servilius Rullus proposed a major distribution of overseas lands to Roman settlers (to the detriment, no doubt, of vast numbers of natives), it was not on moral principle that men like Cicero (in the speeches *de lege agraria*), opposed him and his backers—and the People turned the proposal down because they were persuaded that it was an attack on the absent Pompey.

It was Pompey who was the People's chief hero and benefactor —the man who carried the ideas of the Gracchi in this field to their dazzling conclusion. Compared to him, P. Clodius is merely an isolated brigand. Pompey, of course, was an efficient administrator, who did not abandon the tradition of avoiding excessive administrative commitments. Indeed, he could hardly have done so: for since Sulla the shortage of administrators had been worse than ever. Pompey added territory to Cilicia, organised Bithynia-Pontus (as a single immense province, in order to save personnel) and annexed Syria. Moreover, he was a great founder of cities in all those areas (especially in Bithynia-Pontus, which was short of them), in order to simplify what administration was undertaken.

77

Pompey did not irresponsibly burden the state.[6] In fact, he found the perfect solution.

The separation of *libertas* and *immunitas* had been theoretically possible ever since the Romans first came across it in the Seleucid kingdom; it had occasionally been practised soon after (notably in the case of the tribute imposed on the 'free' Macedonian republics after 167)[7] and was accepted in the organisation of Greece in 146. In Sicily, in the *lex Rupilia* of 132, we find the 'freedom' of the *ciuitates liberae* hedged about with numerous restrictions, all to the economic profit of Rome.[8] In the first century *immunitas* is still often conferred, but as a special favour. However, it seems to have been Pompey who first systematically extended this idea to client princes. His eastern provinces were protected, as had been the tradition, by a layer of client states acting as buffers—tradition, but now first worked out consistently and coherently, and with attention to the frontier as a whole. Pompey (as he himself was to say)[9] found Asia a frontier province and left it in the heart of the empire. With Pompey, the client princes become a real part of the empire (*reichsangehörig*, in Mommsen's word), in a sense in which they never had been before. They now pay tribute to the Roman People. The best-known case is Judaea.[10] How widely the principle applied, we are not told. But there is a well-known fact that may be informative if scrutinised. In his triumph, in addition to rather extravagant claims of victories won and cities founded, and the booty (20,000 talents = 480,000,000 HS) deposited in the Treasury, he asserted that he had raised the *uectigalia* of the Roman People from 200,000,000 HS to 540,000,000 HS.[11] Of course, he is obviously claiming more than his due: Bithynia had been left to the Roman People by will in 74, had been cleared of the enemy by Lucullus and had never again been lost. The fact that it was Pompey who had organised it was, in a way, accidental. However, even so, the figures conclusively show the tribute coming in from 'free' clients. Pompey had added two provinces (plus a strip of Cilicia). These could, by themselves, never have produced 1.7 times as much as all the ten old provinces together. Since he certainly did not increase the revenue from eight of those provinces, which were not concerned in his war, and probably—in view of the state of the country—did not add much to the sum squeezed out of Asia, it follows that a large part of the increase must have been due to a consistent policy of taxing clients. In fact, Pompey had combined the advantages of the traditional policy (freedom from administration) with the chief advantage (as it now was) of imperialism—large revenues. *Vectigalia* were clearly a prime consideration of Pompey, as they had been of C. Gracchus. The People hardly needed Cicero to remind them of what to expect: *vectigalia* now meant their own profits.

Pompey, of course, did not act entirely on political theory. He aimed at keeping the support of the masses, as others did, and he used his chance of doing more to merit it. However, we must see him in his context. He merely carries to extremes what is the common tone in his day. For it is the senators themselves who now take the lead in imperialism in both its principal senses: in exploitation and in aggression. Not surprisingly (in the Roman scheme of things), it is the political class, not the various non-political pressure-groups, that ultimately decides the temper of policy.

The moral effects of the Social and Civil Wars of the decade after 91 have often been noted and need no elaborate treatment. Sulla showed what an unscrupulous and selfish man could now hope to achieve with an army of have-nots closely attached to himself and accustomed to the devastation of Italy—an army resembling its leader in its unhesitating pursuit of its own profit, without any consideration for its country. In Syme's words, 'Sulla could not abolish his own example.'[12] He did try, of course, by administrative checks and safeguards, which added up to a well-conceived and (on paper) promising settlement.[13] But for many reasons—which this is not the place to discuss—he failed. Henceforth it was apparent to anyone who considered the matter with detachment that immense wealth and personal power were within the reach of any man who could obtain a large enough command and, winning the loyalty of his men, was prepared to use it with sufficient lack of scruple.

Worse still, perhaps: Sulla's victory and its consequences proclaimed the bankruptcy of the oligarchy. Sulla had shown that outstanding success could be achieved by ruthless pursuit of self-interest. The hollowness of the aristocratic *res publica* now stood revealed for all to see: the *arcanum imperii* was out, that its rulers and chief beneficiaries no longer seriously believed in it.[14] They had adopted success as their chief criterion. The lesson was bound to sink in sooner or later. Those—and especially ordinary Italians—who had suffered for their loyalty to the *res publica*, although, after all, it had never brought them very much profit, were bound to remember. A generation later it became clear that they and their sons were no longer willing to defend what their rulers had so shamelessly abandoned.

So much for the general effect on the fabric of society. As for the point that particularly concerns us: we have seen that restraints on aggressiveness and expansion and exploitation, in the second century, were not entirely due to moral scruples. Victory and conquest, at any rate, remained in principle desirable ends. The motives that had restrained dreams of personal glory (and enrichment), and of the aggrandisement of the Roman People in accordance with the censors' ritual prayer, had largely been social and political ones. They had gradually ceased to operate. This— as we have seen—was becoming clear even by 89.[15] It was when it was just beginning to appear that the decade of internal war and rebellion smashed the strained fabric. After Sulla, men could seek power and profit without restraint and use it without fear of really firm opposition. Both leaders and men, in the new era, were going to be much more ready for adventure and its rewards.

Pompey was one of the first to learn the new methods—from his father, who had probably been the first to learn them from Sulla,[16] and then under Sulla himself. He turned them first against the lawful government and then against his benefactor Sulla.[17]

Holding *imperium* without a break from 83 to his consulship in 70, he acquired immense *clientelae* and probably immense wealth in all the western provinces; then, after his consulship, he refused to take up a paltry province and waited for his chance. It came in 67/6, and he eagerly seized it. With utter contempt—openly displayed—for his rivals and enemies, he used it to become the patron of the East, which, without consulting Senate or People, he organised like a monarch. The financial profits of this deserve to be stressed.[18] At the end of his Asian campaign Pompey distributed the sum of 16,000 talents (nearly 400,000,000 HS) to his soldiers, who had already received prize money and a great deal of booty in the campaign. 6,000 HS went to each soldier, and the senior officers (we know the names of twenty) received, altogether, the magnificent sum of 100,000,000 HS. It has been shown that centurions probably got twenty times as much as common soldiers and tribunes 120 times as much: a similar distribution in 66 indicates Pompey's scales. If so, it can be calculated that Pompey, at the time of the final distribution, had eight (rather depleted) legions. With these whole-heartedly loyal to him, he would have power such as no man in Rome had ever had, dwarfing the results of the great wars of the second century; not to mention the fact that Sulla had shown to all that the new armies had no thought for the *res publica* and a good deal for those who led and rewarded them.[19]

Not only power due to devoted veterans, but wealth as the basis of a more solid and lasting ascendancy. Marcus Crassus—as we all know—said that no one was wealthy who could not afford to pay for a legion.[20] Marcus Crassus, by display and magniloquence, attained and still retains the reputation of having been the richest man in Rome, at least in his day. In 55 B.C. he made it abundantly clear, before leaving for the East, in order to safeguard the attachments he had won in his absence, which was expected to be prolonged.[21] He sacrificed a tenth of his estate to Hercules (we may be sure that he computed it generously), feasted the whole people, gave every citizen enough to live on for

81

three months, and then announced that he still had 7,000 talents left—no one should be in any doubt that he was a man worth remembering even when away. His fortune, we may say (recognising that we have only his word for it, and that he did nothing to understate the facts), had amounted to about 8,000 talents before the display. Certainly enough to pay for a legion or two: private soldiers, at any rate, were not expensive,[22] and some of the officers would be men whom one had in one's pay in any case, as politicians. Pompey did not advertise his wealth: he had no need to. Yet he could have bought Crassus out without feeling the pinch. The personal profits of the eastern campaign were enormous. As we saw in the case of Nicomedes as early as 89, Roman commanders now expected to be well rewarded for aiding an ally—and in default of money they might accept a promissory note, with regular payment of interest. The 16,000 talents distributed to the army (a quarter of it to the senior officers) give us some idea of what must have been the scale of the commander's own profit. Naturally, investments on this scale could not go into Italian land: there was not enough of it. Fortunately, we can form some idea of what happened to at least some of them.

Cicero, in Cilicia, had to look after the repayment of huge sums owed to Pompey by Ariobarzanes III of Cappadocia. With this man, Pompey had had no personal contact: their only relation was that Pompey had witnessed and approved the transfer of power from his grandfather (Ariobarzanes I) to his father (Ariobarzanes II)—a very indirect and entirely hereditary *beneficium*.[23] There is no doubt that the poor king paid heavily for it. He also had other debts, of which we shall have more to say. Cicero found him besieged *a Pompei procuratoribus sescentis* and trying hard to pay at least the interest that he owed. Thirty-three talents was all he could find per month, and this was in fact not (though it was nearly) enough to cover the interest. Pompey was pleasant and accommodating about it all: *clementer id fert*.[24] No wonder: after all, he hardly needed the capital and, if he got it back, would only have to find a place for reinvesting it. With all prominent Romans in business in a big way, investment opportunities for large sums cannot have been unlimited. Not to mention the advantage of having Ariobarzanes bound to himself by his debt. Pompey knew both business and politics.

A calculation is worth attempting (though necessarily uncertain). At the legal rate of interest (1% per month) this interest means a principal of 3,300 talents—and even if (as is very likely) the great man was not satisfied with the legal maximum, he will hardly have been getting more than twice as much; which still leaves a tidy sum (1,650 talents or 40,000,000 HS) for the indebtedness of a king for whom Pompey, after all, had not done very much. 40,000,000 HS, one might point out, was just enough to provide 100 men with the minimum equestrian census. Unfortunately we cannot tell whether the principal consisted of a sum actually invested in the kingdom or in a promissory note by Ariobarzanes' father for services rendered: we shall not go far wrong if we assume a little of both. We can now imagine what other kings and dynasts, with whom Pompey was in close contact and for whom he had done a great deal, owed him or had paid him. The 10,000 talents that Rabirius Postumus had scraped together for Ptolemy Auletes pale into insignificance in comparison with such sums—not to mention the miserable 8,000 talents that were apparently, even at his own optimistic valuation, the total property of Marcus Crassus.

Then there were the cities. From his province Cicero writes a letter[25] to the governor of Bithynia, which Pompey had organised as a province, asking him to help one Cluvius of Puteoli (of a family of financiers) to collect his debts—which, without official help, he thinks will be a hopeless task; Mylasa, Alabanda, Carian Heraclea, Bargylia and Caunus owe him money, as well as various private individuals. And Cicero adds discreetly: 'Agitur res Cn. Pompei etiam.' Cluvius, as scholars have recognised, was Pompey's financial agent. Drumann summed it all up: 'Mit Schuldscheinen beladen kehrte er nach Italien zurück.'[26] Pompey left the East not only as its patron, but to a considerable extent (and one hard to realise nowadays) literally as its owner. Having assigned it to cities and kings and to the Roman People as far as administration was concerned, he held the mortgage-bonds; and, unlike a modern investor in foreign states, he could be sure that financial control meant political control, as well as a safe income. One can only wonder how much he invested in the numerous cities that he actually founded and where he was worshipped as *ktistes*.

This was business on a grand scale, dwarfing the doings of the *negotiatores* that tend to fill our textbooks. Indeed, as we have seen, these men might well be only the agents of senators. Pompey was the outstanding example; the greatest of the owners of the captive world. Others had their share. We all know about the noble Brutus: Cicero was as shocked as each student still is when it first dawned on him.[27] Brutus' loan to Cyprian Salamis had been made when he was on the island as a private man, and a young man at that (not yet quaestorian), under his uncle M. Cato in 58/6.[28] And since such loans were illegal under the *lex Gabinia*, he charged 48% interest instead of the legal 12% and used two *procuratores* as men of straw. When the Salaminians fell into arrears, one of these men, Scaptius, went to Cicero's predecessor Ap. Claudius, got himself appointed prefect, was given a force of cavalry and proceeded to Cyprus to squeeze money out of the *boule* of Salamis—to such effect that (we are told) five of them starved to death while he held them besieged in the council chamber. But that failed to get him any money, and as a result Cicero had to take cognizance of the affair. He refused to re-appoint Scaptius prefect (we hear incidentally that this gave great offence, since such appointments were regarded as normal and were expected by the great men in Rome interested in such business), but ordered the Salaminians to pay—which they were willing to do, at the legal rate of interest. At this point Scaptius produced a *senatus consultum* that Brutus had procured and that (a) gave legal exemption from the *lex Gabinia* to this whole transaction; and (b) gave similar exemption from the maximum

84

interest rate and ordered the contract to stand as signed (i.e. at 48% instead of 12%). Brutus had assumed open responsibility, when he saw his financial interests endangered, and had evidently had no difficulty in securing the support he wanted. Cicero—who detested the whole affair, but was not willing to be a martyr on behalf of his principles—could do no more than refuse to adjudicate on those terms, and held the matter over for his successor, who would no doubt be more complaisant. This is only an outline of the famous Scaptius affair. But it is clear that even an unusually honest governor could not risk giving serious offence to such as Brutus, who could get senatorial decrees passed in his private interest even in the most disreputable circumstances —not to mention offence to Cicero's own friend Atticus, whose aid Brutus had enlisted, and who 'now begs his dear friend to let Scaptius have a troop of horse—only a little one, just fifty swords—which he felt sure would make the Salaminians see reason'.[29] It is to Cicero's credit that he acted even as he did; and it is clear that few others would have done so.

The amount of the loan cannot be ascertained, since we have no idea how much the Salaminians had been able to pay and for how long. It has been worked out (*exempli gratia*) that, if they never did pay any of the interest due (which is in fact unlikely), the sum borrowed in 56 need have been only 12 talents to give a debt of 200 talents (the actual figure we have) in 50.[30] This is a measure of the profits that were made by senators who—to say the least—did not have a reputation for being unscrupulous: we can imagine what deals an Ap. Claudius or a P. Clodius would be involved in. The most alarming feature of the whole case, however, is the fact that senators—even philosophers among them—were quite prepared to profit from their position in order to put themselves above the law—and that in this they could secure the total and unquestioning support of the Senate as a whole, apparently as a matter of course. Attempts to protect the weak became—as has so often been the result of well-meant social legislation—merely another way of reinforcing the profits of the powerful. The *lex Gabinia*, as far as the provincials were concerned, had only made the terms of loans much worse than they need have been.

The same Brutus had also lent Ariobarzanes money: no doubt (in the light of what we have seen) the King needed it to pay Pompey. But Ariobarzanes really could not pay this additional debt: he was bankrupt and in fear of his life! Even so, Brutus was so persistent that Cicero—who, no doubt, did not want to appear quite unreasonable to his Roman friends and enemies—managed to squeeze no less than 100 talents out of him over six months: proportionately more (he tells us) than Pompey had got (200 talents in six months).[31] Thus, even if the King's debt to Brutus was less than a quarter of what he owed to Pompey, it was quite a sizable sum to owe to a young man barely of quaestorian status. For throughout it is Brutus' age and status that lends terrible significance to his financial manoeuvres.

These are the best-known cases illustrating the way in which senators now profited personally from the empire of the Roman People. They cannot be unique. We know them well because Cicero happened to get involved in them and to write about them, in letters that happen to be preserved. There were many provinces that had no Cicero as their governor, and Cicero's own behaviour, as well as that we see of that of his friends and of the Senate as a whole in these affairs, clearly shows us—as against the attempts of apologists among historians—that we have here stumbled upon what we may regard as widespread and indeed typical. We need hardly add examples from men's actual governorships. Things were obviously very much worse when men of the cast of mind of the honourable Brutus (not to mention worse) had supreme power, without appeal and with little fear of punishment (provided they played the political game in Rome with reasonable care), over the lives and property of a whole province—and when plenty of Roman friends, both in their retinue and at home, expected to be satisfied. As early as 70, the *Verrines* show us what a man could at least hope to get away with—and that a new man, with no claim to nobility. It is human nature—as our own generation has seen—to refuse to believe what seems monstrous and simply to close one's mind to it, however well-attested it may be. There have been those who have urged that Verres was not typical. Yet we have little serious reason for such a view. He was unfortunate in having Cicero as his prosecutor. Had he been luckier at this final stage, there is no real doubt that he would have survived in Rome, reaching honour and a consulship, and perhaps joining in the defence of the Republic against Caesar. Where Cicero speaks for the defence, as he usually did, the case is made to look very different. Yet we can often tell, by his incidental admissions and appeals to precedent, what was regarded as fair and tolerable, and by how much his clients at times surpassed even that very generous measure. No administration in history has ever devoted itself so whole-heartedly to fleecing its subjects for the private benefit of its ruling class as Rome of the last age of the Republic. It is, as usual, the little touches—the references to what did *not* (apparently) arouse astonishment or disgust—that prove most revealing. Thus, before Cicero's governorship the cities of Cyprus had been accustomed to pay 200 talents a year (= 4,800,000 HS) to the Roman governor—i.e. to men as honourable as P. Lentulus Spinther—in order to escape having troops quartered upon them in winter;[32] and that, of course, after M. Porcius Cato, honest and unrelenting, had removed 7,000 talents from the island when it was annexed. We begin to understand why the Salaminians were hopelessly in debt to Cato's young kinsman. All this is well known, to those familiar with the evidence.[33] Laws like the *lex Julia* were probably not even intended to strike at the chief beneficiaries of the system. It is pretty clear that Caesar and his friends ignored them as light-heartedly as anyone.

Naturally, there are now no limits except convenience to calculated aggression by Rome's representatives. Again a small case may be cited as typical, for motives and techniques.[34] M. Scaurus, Pompey's proquaestor, had been left with two legions, *pro praetore*, to look after Syria when Pompey went home. He decided to take up for his own benefit an idea that Pompey, for political reasons, had abandoned and to attack the Arabian dynast Aretas. This man had done homage to Pompey and had given no pretext for war.[35] Yet Scaurus had no scruples about launching his attack. Things did not go as planned, and in the end the young commander had to ask Antipater (of the Jewish dynasty) to mediate and get him the best terms possible. For payment of a lump sum of 300 talents by Aretas, Scaurus withdrew. (He was later, as curule aedile, to boast quite unashamedly of his victory.)[3] We are not told whether the money went to the treasury or into Scaurus' pockets—probably a little of both. But it is clear that Rome's international behaviour had followed the line indicated as early as 89 and had degenerated, at its worst, into highway robbery.

The natural consequences become clear with M. Crassus and C. Caesar. Crassus, in his Parthian war, was merely following in Pompey's footsteps. For Pompey himself—for his part, as we have seen, following in Sulla's—had made an agreement with Phraates of Parthia when he needed his help against Tigranes of Armenia; had calmly broken it when Tigranes submitted to him; had written Phraates an insulting letter when he dared to complain and then crossed the Euphrates and even the Tigris to punish him. In the end Phraates seems to have come to an agreement with Tigranes, and no harm came of it all.[37] We must remember that, only a generation earlier, Sulla, while behaving with characteristic insolence towards the envoy of the Parthian king, had never had any intention of breaking the agreement he had made with him.[38] The difference is apparent. And Pompey's actions gave Crassus his idea. Parthia was clearly just another client state, and one whose insolence had shown that it had not been sufficiently humbled; and M. Crassus, as clearly, was the man to do it, to his own political and (no doubt) economic advantage: the wealth that Pompey had gained in the East can safely be assumed to have been as powerful a motive as his glory. In 55, after obtaining the province of Syria, he invaded Parthian territory without pretext or declaration of war.[39] The result was Carrhae, and a dangerous conflict ended (temporarily) only by Augustus. For once arrogance and greed had found their nemesis. But it was Rome's good fortune that Parthia, essentially unstable, was in no position to take advantage of her own strength and Rome's weakness—and that no better opponent remained. We have seen the attested hatred for Rome among the subjects she was exploiting. But they remained impotent.

Very different, of course, is the story of C. Caesar, the greatest brigand of them all, applying and perfecting the lessons of Pompey both at home and abroad, with a single-mindedness not weakened (as in Pompey's case) by scruples about traditional forms or by desire for the approval of his peers. The sweet reasonableness of the *Commentaries* cannot disguise the fact that Caesar started a major foreign war and then a civil one—for a variety of reasons, as we all know, but chiefly (as he at times comes close to admitting) for his personal glory and profit. We know how well he succeeded. Unfortunately we have no letters of Cicero's to give us a detailed idea of Caesar's profits in Gaul and their investment. In this as in other respects he was more fortunate than his rival. But we have some facts, above all the millions spent to 'buy' friends in Rome: an 'enormous wage'[40] for the tribune Curio (the figures vary from ten to sixty million sesterces);[41] 1,500 talents (36,000,000 HS) for the consul L. Paullus;[42] large—though ultimately ineffectual—loans to Cicero (who, as we have seen before, behaved in ways that were unintelligible to his less scrupulous contemporaries);[43] not to mention his well-known *liberalitas* to those who joined him in Gaul, from L. Balbus and the 'ghastly Mamurra'[44] to Cicero's young friend, the lawyer C. Trebatius Testa, to whose prospects of quick enrichment Cicero never fails to refer in their surviving correspondence.[45] At his triumph in 46—by which time (admittedly) he had conquered not only Gaul, but the world—Caesar, in addition to lavish banquets on 22,000 *triclinia* and gifts to all citizens, not to

mention games such as no one had ever seen before, paraded booty
worth 65,000 talents and gold crowns weighing 20,414 lbs in the
procession, and gave each soldier 5,000 *denarii* (Pompey in Asia
had been able to afford only 1,500). These figures are official and
well-attested.[46] And in view of Caesar's actions, there is no
doubt that, at least in some cases, the opportunity for such profits
had been deliberately sought and created. This is the striking
difference between the late and the middle Republic.

It has recently been argued[47] that Caesar was not really an
imperialist: he did nothing aggressive at the start of the Gallic
War, but was merely led from one thing to another; and at the
end of it all, after (admittedly) much cruelty and plundering, he
merely created client states (under the supervision of the Aedui
and Arverni) rather than a province, and did not tax Gaul too
heavily. The points are worth making, and repeating in our
context: there is much about Caesar that can fairly be called traditional, much that was dictated by circumstances rather than deliberately willed. Yet there is another side. That Caesar did not
aim at the conquest of the whole of Gaul at the very start of the
war is certain; but no less certainly, he was not merely led on by
circumstances, but, with callous brutality and treachery (surpassing the worst that Roman commanders had done in second-
century Spain), seized every chance of further conquest, never
stopping until (by 57) conquest was total. After that, of course,
he could no longer withdraw, even if he had wished to (which
there is no reason to suppose). Moreover, he had learnt all
Pompey's lessons. There was no need to saddle Rome with the
direct administration of a vast tribal area, as had been done—
with such dire consequences—in second-century Spain. Pompey
had found the happy solution: they could be taxed without being
governed. Admittedly, ten million *denarii* does not seem a heavy
tax. Caesar, at the time when he imposed it, had to count on the
loyalty of newly-won Gaul in his rear during the civil war that
he could foresee. But let us not go too far in depreciating the
figure. We must not be misled by the vast figures with which

we have lately been dealing. The sum was, we must remember, one eighth of what Rome, only twenty years earlier, had been getting out of ten provinces.[48] It was not an exceptionally light burden for a province that had been bled white and had been subjected to what we nowadays call genocide during eight years of war[49]—and a province that had made many private Roman fortunes.

After victory, of course, Caesar is the great imperialist, able to deal with the conquered world without being distracted by thoughts of opposition abroad or rivalry at home. Annexation (as in Africa Nova), semi-annexation (as in Gaul), client statuses of various sorts (as frequently in the East)—all can be used and altered as he thinks fit. Colonisation becomes more lavish than ever before. Since he had so little time, we do not know what he meant to do in the end. Nor, of course, did he. When he died, he was preparing another Parthian war; for his policy had come to a dead end: 'Er wollte den Knoten zerhauen, indem er in den Krieg zog' (as Gelzer has put it).[50] The robber barons bred by the removal of the traditional restraints that had governed both personal behaviour and public policy had gained wealth and glory that had previously been only a distant dream; they had gained it both for Rome and for themselves, asserting *uirtus* without a care for morality or even expediency. They had raised an astonishing structure, founded on ambition, greed and lust for power, bringing out the worst that had perhaps been implicit in the Roman way of life from the start; and they had killed one another off in the process, until the last and greatest of them, *felix opportunitate mortis*, was slaughtered by men no better than himself, for the sake of ideals that they themselves no longer either practised or believed in—in time to prevent him from plunging into what would almost certainly have been defeat, and quite possibly chaos even worse than what in fact followed.

We have had to stress the horror, the degeneracy, the degradation. They do not always appear as clearly in the books of benevolent historians as the glories of the Ciceronian age—the

91

freedom, the tolerance, the *magna ingenia* and the gracious living. If the Roman empire had broken up before 31 B.C., what historian would have shed a tear for it? We should all have hastened to point the moral of the inevitable nemesis.

Why, in fact, it did *not* break up, in spite of all that we have seen—why, in the end, Augustus managed to save and restore it; to subdue the explosion of energy (by then almost exhausted) that had made Rome great and burnt it out; and how, incidentally, he came to realise, after trials and errors of his own, that *imperium sine fine* (in both a spatial and a moral sense) was not given to any man or people—why and how this came about, instead of the general disintegration that was expected by many at the time and would certainly not have surprised the historian, that is a very large and quite different question. We have glimpsed some parts of the answer: good fortune for a start (as in the long life of Augustus); and some Roman qualities that, on the whole, survived until they could play their decisive part: the tenacity that had many times lost battles and won wars; the *fides* that consistently rewarded friends and never sacrificed them to placate an enemy; the network of personal alliances with the ruling elements everywhere that opened to them the hope of sharing in the power and the glory of the Roman name, and ultimately, of full acceptance into the ruling race.[51] They are qualities that we do not put high on the scale of moral values. But they are qualities that make for survival.

Perhaps there is also a lesson we have learnt as historians of Rome. The study of the Roman Republic—and that of the Empire to a considerable degree—is basically the study, not of its economic development, or of its masses, or even of great individuals: it is chiefly the study of its ruling class.

NOTES

1. In a justly famous article W. Capelle (*Klio* 1932, 86) investigated the development of a Greek (and particularly Stoic) tradition that provided a justification for Roman imperialism on an ethical plane, after the familiar pattern (ultimately derived from Aristotle, who applied it *i.a.* to slavery) that it is better for some to be ruled by their superiors. Some of this tradition—which, as Capelle argues, was first formulated by Panaetius in the second century B.C. and passed on to the 'Scipionic circle'—not unexpectedly recurs in Cicero's philosophical writings, e.g. the *de re publica*. Such ideas naturally and inevitably fitted into the aristocratic *Weltanschauung* that had evolved the concept of *clientela*; and I am not unaware of this concept and its importance. As for the Greek influence, it seems to me that—here as elsewhere—Roman aristocrats merely acquired a certain skill at formulating Roman ideas in Greek language; and as far as the concepts are concerned, it is largely the Greek tradition that adapts itself to that of the Roman aristocracy. It is chiefly for this reason (and not through ignorance) that, both in my *Foreign Clientelae* and here, I have preferred to concentrate on the Roman tradition and not on the Greek language—though I do not underestimate the importance of the latter, especially in making Roman rule acceptable to the East and in providing—as philosophers are given to doing, now as in antiquity—an acceptable basis for the facts of power. Perhaps this approach is incomplete. But it will at least avoid the obvious traps of its opposite: it will be remembered that Capelle ends up by convincing himself that the idea of a *iustum bellum* (in fact enshrined in autochthonous Italic ritual) was a contribution of Hellenistic philosophy (and of Panaetius in particular) to Roman thinking (*op. cit.* 112f. and especially 97): Augustus' 'nulli genti per iniuriam bello inlato' (*RG* 26, 3) is described as 'bei einem Römer sehr auffallend' and said to refer to the 'Erweiterung der Grenzprovinzen'—in fact it is strangely (one might say) limited to *Italy* and is clearly a survival of fetial ritual. It is perhaps better to leave Greek theory out of the reckoning; though a major task remains to be done in determining its true place in enabling the Hellenistic world to accept the fact of Roman power.

2. This is now a commonplace, especially since Gelzer's epoch-making *Die Nobilität der römischen Republik* (1912: now in his *Kleine Schriften* i (1962)—a fitting jubilee occasion).

93

3. Mommsen, *RG* 12 (1920) i 781 *et al.*
4. On this and what follows, see *FC*, especially 73f., and *SGRH* 112f. ('Rome and Antiochus the Great').
5. On this see now J. Briscoe, *JRS* 1964, 66f.
6. On this and what follows, see *FC* 96f. (with references).
7. 142B.C.: see Val. Max. iv 1, 10. The fact of the change must be excepted, even if the anecdote is fictitious. (On this, see now Astin, *Scipio Aemilianus* (1967), 325f.)
8. On the famous debate, see especially Gelzer, *Kl. Schr.* ii (1963) 39f.: it became a favourite of moralising Greek historiography. We have recently been (very properly) warned by a careful student of Roman policy against overestimating the political importance of the debate at the time (W. Hoffmann, *Historia* 1960, 340). In so far as Scipio defended Carthage in the Senate, he would do so chiefly as its patron, advancing whatever arguments would best support his case.
9. It was Rostovtzeff who most clearly drew the distinction and warned against excluding 'hegemonial imperialism' from our considerations: 'Imperialism does not always involve the intention of acquiring an increase of territory. The desire for political hegemony . . . cannot but be regarded as a form of imperialism' (*SEHHW* i 70).
10. On Spain (where there is more—but not much—information) see, for a general outline, C. H. V. Sutherland, *The Romans in Spain* (1939); and, for a more thorough treatment, vol. ii of the monumental *Historia de España* (ed. R. Menéndez Pidal, 1935), Part I (by P. Bosch Gimpera and P. Aguado Bleye), chapters II-IV.
11. This point of view has recently been strongly put by H. Braunert, *Historia* 1964, 8, and should certainly be borne in mind throughout. But he finally refuses to recognise the existence of the equilibrium as such, and in this I cannot follow him.
12. Pol. iii 22-4. The first is dated by Polybius—we do not know on what evidence—to the first year of the Republic. It must certainly have been very old, and the date may well be correct.
13. This thesis is very effectively argued in two works by the Danish scholar A. Afzelius: *Die römische Eroberung Italiens* (1942) and *Die römische Kriegsmacht während der Auseinandersetzung mit den hellenistischen Grossmächten* (1944).
14. On the epoch-making speech of Appius Claudius the Blind, which Cicero still read (whether or not in an authentic version), see A. Garzetti, *Athenaeum* 1947, 219f.
15. I have treated these extensively in *FC*, particularly 25-54.
16. This interpretation, which I first advanced in 1952 (see *SGRH* 22f.), was developed in *FC* 58-66. It has not—to my knowledge—been disproved by any of the numerous writers who have added to the vast bibliography on the problem of the outbreak of the Second Macedonian War. See, e.g.,

B. Ferrua, *Le origini della II guerra Macedonica* (1960), in which all views up to that time are fully (though not always accurately) summarised.

17. On this, see *SGRH* 126f. (with notes).
18. I hope to develop my views on it in a forthcoming book on *Roman Provincial Administration in the Republic*.
19. On the increasing shortage of manpower, see especially E. Gabba, *Athenaeum* 1949, 175f.
20. See *FC* 166 (with references).
21. Livy xliii 2.
22. See *MRR* i 450–1 (with n. 2).
23. See the cases (to mention only a few) of M. Furius Crassipes (xxxix 3); M. Claudius Marcellus (*ibid.* 54); A. Manlius Vulso (xli 10–1); Q. Fulvius Flaccus (xlii 3); M. Popillius Laenas and C. Popillius Laenas (xlii 7–12; 21; 22); C. Cassius Longinus (xliii 1). The worst (and perhaps decisive) example was Ser. Sulpicius Galba, the perfidious murderer and brilliant orator (see *ORF*[3], no. 19). My discussion is in no way intended to deny the obvious connection between his acquittal by a *iudicium populi* and the Senate's decision that such enquiries had better be taken into more competent hands in future.
24. *MRR* i 459. See W. S. Ferguson, *JRS* 1921, 97f. He notices the probability of a connection with the imminent creation of new provinces, but strangely tries to explain the annexations by the successful passing of the *lex Calpurnia*. I cannot accept E. S. Gruen's attempt to ascribe the *lex Calpurnia* chiefly to the Senate's desire not to see such cases dealt with by the *Populus*; though he is undoubtedly right in drawing attention to the fact that the *Populus* had just acquitted Ser. Galba. (See n. 23, above.)
25. On the *poena repetundarum* and its development, see A. N. Sherwin-White, *PBSR* 1949, 5, and *JRS* 1952, 43 (successfully controverting M. I. Henderson). E. S. Gruen's forthcoming book (which he has kindly allowed me to see) throws much new light on the political implications of *repetundae* laws in the late Republic.
26. For these events, see *MRR* i 458.
27. See my discussion of this in *Athenaeum* 1956, 104; cf. *SGRH* 172f.
28. Cic. 2 *Verr.* ii 94f. Yet the Senate renewed Verres' *imperium* after this.
29. See, e.g., *Geschichte von Numantia* (1933) 7–9; *CAH* viii (1930) 324f.
30. On Galba, see *RE*, s.v. 'Sulpicius' 58; *ORF*[3], no. 19.
31. *RE*, s.v. 'Hostilius' 18. The praetorship is not registered in *MRR*. I feel no doubt that his quaestor Ti. Gracchus was acting in good faith.
32. See Kiechle, *Historia* 1958, 129f.
33. This is clear from the brutal frankness of the Roman treaty with the Aetolian League: see *FC* 56f. and, for further references to discussions of the epigraphic fragment, *SEG* xvi (1959) 110; xvii (1960) 75. On this treaty and its implications the excellent work of G. A. Lehmann, *Untersuchungen über die historische Glaubwürdigkeit des Polybios* (1967) must now be consulted; though his apologetic tendency should not always be followed.

34. On the fetial law, see *RE*, s.v. 'fetiales', especially coll. 2261f.
35. See McDonald and Walbank, *JRS* 1937, 180f.; cf. *FC* 66f.
36. As has been suggested by S. I. Oost, *AJP* 1954, 147.
37. On this, see now D. C. Earl, *The Moral and Political Tradition of Rome* (1967).
38. On *uirtus*, see Earl, *op. cit.* and *The Political Thought of Sallust* (1961) 18f. For the 'mana' view, A. N. van Omme (a pupil of Wagenvoort), *Virtus* (Diss. Utrecht, n.d.).
39. These are conveniently printed in *ILLRP* i 177–86. The numbers here quoted are numbers 309, 310, 313, all of the second century.
40. See Cicero's attacks on L. Piso on this score in the *In Pisonem* and elsewhere. Clearly, this was expected to be acceptable to readers.
41. See *FC*, especially chapters I and VII (with references). The recognition of this, as of so much else, goes back (in its modern form) principally to Gelzer's *Nobilität* (cited n. 2).

CHAPTER II

1. Notably by Rostovtzeff in his *SEHHW* and *SEHRE*. On all this, see now the illuminating discussion by P. A. Brunt, in *Second International Conference of Economic History, 1962* (1965) 117–49, which unfortunately I saw only some time after these lectures were delivered. It will be clear from what follows that, as usual, I agree with all his main points, even where he takes pains to make clear that his approach differs from mine. His article has made it easier for me to keep these notes short.
2. Livy xxxviii 44 (187 B.C.). Cf. Frank, *RI* 279f., arguing that this provision is exceptional. We have no means of knowing; though it was certainly not universal.
3. See Rostovtzeff, *SEHHW* ii 787f., 1267.
4. See the instructive collection of material (especially names) by J. Hatzfeld, *Les Trafiquants italiens dans l'Orient hellénique* (1919) and in *BCH* 1912, 5–218; and compare the useful discussion by Frank, *RI* 284f. A. J. N. Wilson (*Emigration from Italy in the Republican Age of Rome*, 1966) has shown that Hatzfeld underestimated the number of Italians on Delos who might be Roman citizens. The whole matter needs renewed study, in the light of what facts we possess. See now Donati, *Epigraphica* 1965, 3.
5. The popularity of this term is, of course, due to K. J. Beloch's great work, *Der italische Bund unter Roms Hegemonie* (1880), which, despite its great merits, introduced confusion by seeing Rome's Italian alliance in terms of a confederacy or a Greek symmachy. It has done a great deal of harm, even leading scholars into talking of federal instruments and institutions, where in fact there were none.

6. See my treatment of this in *FC* 176f., showing how the proposal for enfranchisement arose out of the Gracchan agrarian schemes. This, of course, is not to assert that the commissioners, for their own purposes, created a demand that would otherwise not have arisen—no one has ever said this. But it is plain fact that it does not appear in politics until they introduce it, and Appian (*b.c.* i 21) rightly stresses this.

7. Livy xlv 18. The censors of 169/8 (*MRR* i 424) had had trouble with the *publicani*.

8. Frank, *RI* 209f. As I have suggested, in this connection (*FC* 97) and others, we must also remember, before we search for elaborate legal concepts, that it could seem nothing less than insane to Romans to give up collecting contributions that people were accustomed to paying and therefore willing to pay. It is the *reduction* that is surprising and worthy of comment. We do not know whether the Macedonian tribute originally had a time-limit.

9. Pliny, *n.h.* xxxiii 56. Indirect taxes to some extent took their place.

10. For a description of this, see the discussion of *L'or hellénistique* in Bloch-Carcopino, *Hist. rom.* (ed. Glotz) ii 63f.

11. Cic. *rep.* iii 16; 'nos uero iustissimi homines, qui transalpinas gentes oleam et uitem serere non sinimus, quo pluris sint nostra oliueta nostraeque uineae.'

12. *SEHRE*² i 22; ii 548, n. 17: eloquent on economic 'parallels', but ignoring the actual text and its meaning.

13. *RI* 280f. (Cf. *ESAR* i 172f.)

14. For the great care taken by Cicero and Atticus over the historical setting of the dialogues, see the careful investigation of the Commission of 146 in *Att.* xiii. (See my study of this in *Mélanges M. Renard* (forthcoming).)

15. See, e.g., Cic. *l. agr.* ii 76, 86f.

16. References *MRR* i 467.

17. Pol. xxxix 3f. For a detailed survey of what is known of the organisation of Greece after 146 B.C., see S. Accame, *Il dominio romano in Grecia* (1946).

18. See *Lex Agraria* (*FIRA*² 8) 79f.

19. The precedent was the will of Ptolemy 'Physcon', made when he feared assassination. See *FC* 109f. (with references) and cf. Luzzatto, *SDHI* 1941, 259f.

20. See *FC* 174. My interpretation has been accepted by D. C. Earl, *Tiberius Gracchus* (1963).

21. This is clear—though not explicitly stated—in Plutarch's account: it was alleged that the Pergamene envoy had brought Tiberius a diadem (*Ti. Gr.* 14). The kernel of truth in this story (the allegation was made by a respectable and responsible man) is, of course, that his high-handed dealings with the envoy, who stayed at his house as his client, aroused resentment and suspicion.

22. Cf. *OGIS* 435.

23. *MRR* i 499. (But the departure of the mission is probably to be put in 133.) The era of the province of Asia later dated from 134/3, the year of Attalus' death. Indeed, it is difficult to see how else it could have been dated after

annexation. There could hardly be a gap in the record. Our earliest evidence on the era comes from the first century.

24. See pp. 29f.
25. *MRR* i 504, 506, 507, 509.
26. Livy xxxvii 2, 3; 58, 6f. On the nomenclature of the Roman provinces see P. P. Spranger, *Untersuchungen zu den Namen der römischen Provinzen* (1955). He fails to explain the nomenclature of the military *prouinciae*.
27. Livy xliii 1.
28. App. *Mithr.* 7; Livy, *per.* xciii; *et al.*
29. *MRR* i 518, 521; 525, 529.
30. For the war, see *MRR* i 510–24 (*passim*). It has become an accepted modern myth that a province (in the full sense of the word) was established by Cn. Domitius Ahenobarbus; and its 'frontiers' have even been specified. I protested against this in *FC* 264, n. 3 and 287f. and have argued the case at greater length in *Mélanges Piganiol* (1966), 901f.: there is certainly no actual reference to such a province in any ancient source, and there are good reasons for denying its existence.
31. Cf. Strabo iv 1,5 (180 C). See my discussion (*art. cit.*, last note).
32. Cic. *Font.* 13. On the date, see H. B. Mattingly, *Mélanges Grenier* (1962) 1159f., almost decisive against the traditional view. The numismatic evidence is at present still ambiguous, though it is becoming likely that the coins will have to be put nearer 118 than Mattingly thought. (I should like to thank Mr Michael Crawford for informing me of some important results of his careful sorting of the Republican coinage.) L. Crassus' speech cited by Cic. *Br.* 160 and obviously (as Mattingly has shown) to be dated some years *after* 118 seems in fact to have been delivered, not on the occasion of the proposal to found the colony, but in opposition to a move to dissolve the colony already founded. This is made clear by the more precise reference in *Cluent.* 140, which must surely refer to the same famous speech: as one of the official founders of the colony, Crassus had a primary right and duty to oppose such a move. For the move itself, we may compare the case of Junonia, founded in 123 and disbanded in 121 (*MRR* i 519, n. 5, corrected in *Suppl.* 53; *ibid.*, 521, under 'Tribunes of the Plebs'). But it is unlikely that a fully established colony would be disbanded five years after its foundation. Since 113 is the most probable date for Crassus' speech, the coins of the Narbo foundation should in any case be somewhat later than 118.
33. Cic. *Br.* 160.
34. Strabo iv 1, 12 (186 C).
35. For this story, see Strabo iv 1,8 (183 C).
36. We do not know precisely when and by whom. As I have pointed out (*art. cit.*, n. 30 above), the absence of attested governors at the time of the first German attack strikingly contrasts with their attested presence at various times in the nineties.

37. 'Sallustio e la guerra di Giugurta', *Problemi di Storia Antica* (1932) 187. Cf. my discussion of Numidia in *FC* 192f.
38. On this, see Sall. *Jug.* 9f.
39. Some of them are known (*MRR* i 491); but there must have been many more. One wonders where M. Scaurus himself was in 134/3: he was old enough to be an officer, perhaps just old enough to be quaestor. His selection to head the mission to Jugurtha, as well as the later suspicion of bribery, may be due to pre-existing personal links with Jugurtha—so well known that no one has bothered to inform us of them—no less than to his official standing.
40. Sall. *Jug.* l.c.
41. This term (used by De Sanctis) still seems to me at least useful: see my Introduction, pp. viif.
42. Sall. *Jug.* 26.
43. Varro *ap.* Non. Marc. p. 728 L. This famous judgment is, of course, vastly exaggerated: as I have often tried to point out, the Equites as an order had no political ambitions (though individual members might have). But it is literally true in that C. Gracchus had given the non-political part of the upper class a recognised part in the government and thereby recognised political power. That political differences between the two orders ensued, no one who knows the history of extortion legislation down to 70 can deny; though we must avoid the common error of interpreting them in terms of an attempt by the Equites to oust the Senate from its traditional duties and privileges.
44. *MRR* i 546. The connection between the Commission (with the *iudicium* that followed) and the Gracchan troubles has been convincingly traced by D. C. Earl, *Latomus* 1965, 532f.
45. Sall. *Jug.* 85.
46. For the settlement, see *CAH* ix 130. There is no good evidence for the view that a 'buffer state' was created between the two parts.
47. Sall. *Jug.* 16.
48. Pol. xxi 11, 6f.
49. On the contrary, one strand of the varied tradition even tells us that he was acclaimed by his very enemies (Livy, *per.* lxviii). The conventional charge of massive bribery can be confidently ignored: the man who had just saved Italy had no need for it. The story was spread—much later—by his principal enemy P. Rutilius Rufus, and even Plutarch, usually far from critical of good men, is unwilling to accept it (*Mar.* 28).

CHAPTER III

1. S. I. Oost, *CP* 1963, 11f. (I have discussed some matters relating to Cyrene in *JRS* 1965, 110f.) A dedication by the Cyrenaeans to C. Claudius Pulcher

(*cos.* 92), apparently dated in his consulship, has just been excellently published by L. Gasperini, *Quaderni di Archeologia della Libia* v (1967) 53f. Gasperini (probably rightly) argues from this and the dedication to Aeglanor (see *SEG* xx, 1960, 729) that the cities must have been 'freed' by the Senate (in accordance with the will of Ptolemy) and that relations between Rome and them were good up to this time; he also seems right in moving the tyranny mentioned by Plutarch (see Oost, *op. cit.*) down to a slightly later date (after 91?), when Rome was too busy to interfere. It will, however, be clear that I do not agree with his statement (p. 57) that the Senate, by its refusal to annex, 'alienated . . . the sympathies of the middle class'. It is quite possible that the period of turbulence began before the actual tyrannies—which are more often a symptom of trouble than its beginning —and that the merit for which C. Claudius is honoured was some official action (probably a *senatus consultum*, which, as consul, he would initiate, or a letter written in his official capacity) attempting a peaceful settlement of the situation as it had developed up to this point. This, as we have seen in the case of Jugurtha, would be normal Senate practice where no intervention by armed force was deemed necessary.

2. Pliny, *n.h.* xix 39: 'publice' certainly cannot refer to a payment of tribute and is most naturally taken as meaning (as so often) 'at the public expense'.

3. p. 22 above.

4. The precedents of Ptolemy 'Physcon', Attalus III and Ptolemy Apion have been noted. That the testament is that of Alexander I (made in 88) and not that of Alexander II (some eight years later) is argued in *RhM* 1967, 178f., where the whole matter is discussed in detail.

5. For the Egyptian problem in the sixties, see especially Cicero's speeches *de lege agraria*.

6. See *Athenaeum* xxxiv (1956) 104f.

7. See *ibid.* and *SGRH* 157f.

8. On this and what follows, see my discussion in *SGRH*—where (however) I failed to see the obvious explanation for the partial rehabilitation of Marius.

9. Plut. *Mar.* 31.

10. On this and what follows, see *SGRH*, l.c. (n. 7). For the precedent (the mission to Jugurtha) see Sall. *Jug.* 25.

11. Livy, *per.* lxxxiii; Plut. *Sulla* 22; *et al.* On this peace, see *SGRH* 225f. (with notes).

12. *MRR* ii 64, 70, 77.

13. Augustus, *RG* 27, 1. For Sulla's action on Egypt, see p. 30 above.

14. *History of Rome* (tr. W. P. Dickson, 1880–1) iii 368f. This is still the only valid explanation for the numbers fixed by Sulla.

15. *MRR* ii 74, 77, 84 (misdated: see *Suppl.* 47).

16. Sen. *br. vit.* 13, 8. On the *pomoerium* and its ritual, see *RE*, s.v., where the evidence is collected and discussed.

17. Strabo v 1, 11, *fin.* (=217 C). Mommsen first made this connection (*l.c.*

(n. 14)), and it is generally accepted (e.g. Nissen, *Ital. Landesk.* i (1883) 76; Thomsen, *Italic Regions* (1947) 113).

18. *MRR* ii 87; 88, n. 5; 90; 92, n. 6; 99; 105. See Syme, *Buckler Studies* (1939) 299f.
19. See my discussion in *FC* 140 and *art. cit.* (n. 1).
20. Sall. *hist.* ii 45 and 47 M. Sallust's dislike for Cotta, palpable in the speech, has been confirmed by Dr G. Perl's work on the Berlin palimpsest (see n. 22). See now Perl, *Philologus* 1967, 137f.
21. Cic. 2 *Verr.* iii 163; v 52.
22. Not a suitable person, according to Sallust. (This appears from a new reading of the palimpsest at this point, which Dr G. Perl intends to publish and has kindly communicated to me; cf. his views in *Philologus* 1965, 75f.)
23. For what follows, see Reynolds, *JRS* 1962, 97f., and my discussion, *art. cit.* (n. 1).
24. Ferrero, *Greatness and Decline of Rome* i (tr. Zimmern, 1907) 149f. On Lucullus, see above all Plutarch's *Life.*
25. The election: Plut. *Luc.* 6; Cic. *parad.* v 40. The battle: Plut. *Luc.* 27, *fin.*-28. The comment by the philosopher Antiochus was almost certainly written after Pompey's eastern campaigns and not in ignorance of them.
26. Plut. *Luc.* 30f. Gelzer (*RE*, s.v. 'Licinius', col. 400) rightly rejects it.
27. I suggested this identification of Sulla's unnamed quaestor (App. *b.c.* i 57) in a lecture to the Roman Society in 1960 (see now *SGRH* 220).
28. Plut. *Luc.* 35.
29. *MRR* ii 129; 155.
30. For Syria, see Downey, *History of Antioch* 139f.
31. See Syme, *Roman Revolution* (1939) 32f.
32. See *MRR* ii 215.
33. On this, see Gelzer, *Caesar*[6] (1960) 118f.
34. Plut. *Cato Maior* 21. Some of the Italians on Delos may be freedmen (and their descendants) of senatorial families. (See n. 4, p. 96 above.)
35. On the *lex Claudia* (*MRR* i 238) much has been written, some of it pure fantasy. There is not enough evidence to make it probable that a fully satisfactory explanation will ever be found. But, as against the various combinations of supposed party interests and differences, the statement in the text seems an unexceptionable minimum.
36. Livy xliii 2.
37. See p. 48 above.
38. Whatever the phrase means. (See now Brunt, *op. cit.* (ch. 2, n. 1), reviving the old suggestion that it is meant to be a 'party' label.)
39. Pliny, *n.h.* xxxvi 116. I tried to explain this phrase (tentatively and with no pretensions to finality) in the political context of the nineties, in *Athenaeum* 1956, 120, n. 3. For the trial, see Asc. 21 C.
40. Dio, fr. 97 B.
41. I have developed this aspect of the trial in *SGRH* 39 and 55 (with notes).

CHAPTER IV

1. See pp. 21f. above.
2. Plut. *Ti. Gr.* 9.
3. Cic. *Tusc. disp.* iii 48.
4. Cic. *off.* ii 72.
5. On this enormity, see especially Vell. ii 7: 'in legibus Gracchi inter perniciosissimas numerarim quod extra Italiam colonias posuit.'
6. p. 24 above.
7. Diod. xxxv 25.
8. On the *lex Hieronica*, amply described and discussed in the *Verrines*, see Carcopino, *La Loi de Hiéron et les Romains* (1914)—still the standard modern work. Hiero's system was based on Ptolemaic experience, as adapted to a region which (unlike Egypt) consisted largely of Greek cities. (See Bengtson, *Kokalos* 1964/5, 319f.) The Romans were not capable of introducing this sophisticated scheme beyond Sicily, though they did spread it over the whole of the island after annexing all of it.
9. Cic. *imp. Cn. Pomp.* 14: 'nam ceterarum prouinciarum uectigalia, Quirites, tanta sunt ut eis ad ipsas prouincias tuendas uix contenti esse possimus. Asia uero tam opima est ac fertilis ut et ubertate agrorum at uarietate fructuum et magnitudine pastionis et multitudine earum rerum quae exportentur facile omnibus terris antecellat.'
10. Cic. *Flacc.* 91. Whether these are local or provincial taxes makes no great difference for our purpose.
11. App. *b.c.* i 22. The organisation imposed by Aquillius, through all troubles and changes, continued officially to be the basic law of Asia and is attested as such even in the time of Augustus (Strabo xiv 1, 39, 646C).
12. That *publicani* were conspicuously active in the new province as early as 129 B.C. (*IGRRP* iv 262; see now R. K. Sherk, *GRBS* 1966, 361f.) cannot be charged to the debit of C. Gracchus! On the other hand, it is worth considering that this case may have played its part in making him formulate his plans for provincial reform: it showed that, unlike Roman magistrates and promagistrates, *publicani* were subject to the effective scrutiny of the Senate and (as far as could be foreseen) not likely to become an uncontrolled menace.
13. See Cic. 2 *Verr.* iii 12. It is a fitting commentary on the quality of our sources for this period that the Asian tax law is nowhere set out for us in detail in the main tradition. Apart from Cicero's passing reference (l.c.), we can only glean scattered information about its working in the age of Cicero himself—we do not know how close, by then, it was to its original form.
14. See especially *Athenaeum* 1956, 104f. and *SGRH* 157f.
15. E.g. *Verr.* i 38: 'nullo, iudices, equite Romano iudicante ne tenuissima quidem suspicio acceptae pecuniae ob rem iudicandam'; *ibid.* 51: 'qua lege [Acilia] populus Romanus de pecuniis repetundis optimis iudiciis seuerissimisque iudicibus usus est.' These passages, incidentally, still seem to me to

make the traditional view that the *lex Acilia* was C. Gracchus' law in its final form quite certain, and the further identification with the epigraphical *Lex Repetundarum* highly probable. Nothing that I have read on the subject in the years since I wrote on it (in *AJP* 1954, 374f.)—and I hope I have read everything published up to the end of 1967—has given me any reason to change my mind on this aspect of the question. Nicolet's complicated speculations on the text and substance of C. Gracchus' law (*L'Ordre éq.* i 475–515) are quite unacceptable.

16. Cic. 2 *Verr*. iii 184; iv 22: the manuscripts do not quite agree, and Vell. ii 8,1 gives a different figure. But the range is narrow and Cicero's stress on the amazing smallness of the figure surely justified.

17. Most of the (exceedingly numerous) sources are collected in Greenidge-Clay, *Sources*,[2] 125–7. I am glad to see that on the effectiveness of C. Gracchus' jury law Nicolet has once again independently reached the same conclusion.

18. See Sallust's insistence on the change made by Q. Metellus in the conduct of the war and his account of Metellus' initial successes.

19. Metellus' trial *repetundarum*, at which equestrian jurors refused to insult him by actually inspecting his books (Cic. *Balb*. 11), must come after his return from Numidia. Sallust's claim that he had a friendly reception as soon as he reached Rome (*Jug*. 88,1) is worth no more than many another of that author's assertions, notably his famous description (*Jug*. 63,3f.) of Marius' brilliant and unhampered early career. Metellus' triumph was delayed until early 106 (*Inscr. It.* xiii 1, 84 and 561: date unknown, except that it was not later than August 1st), i.e. certainly for several months; and this triumphal *agnomen* appears to have been due to the Senate (Vell. ii 11). The trial mentioned by Cicero is conventionally placed after his (unrecorded) praetorian command; but such extreme deference seems quite inappropriate in the case of a mere praetorian, however distinguished in birth.

20. See p. 24 above.

21. *vir. ill.* 73.

22. See the small, but useful, selection of sources in Greenidge-Clay, *Sources*[2], 94.

23. *vir. ill.* 23. For Gaul, see App. *b.c.* i 29—not quite clear as to which Gaul, but by his wording apparently suggesting Transalpina (which also makes better sense politically: on this, see *FC* 208f.).

24. I have argued this in *FC* 208f.

25. For Aleria in Corsica, see Pliny, *n.h.* iii 80; Sen. *ad Helv.* 9. On the whole subject, particularly in the later Republic, see Vittinghoff, *Röm. Kolonisation und Bürgerrechtspolitik* (1951) 54. This kind of settlement was soon so much taken for granted that we hear of it only by accident or in special cases (e.g. Caes. *b.c.* iii 4).

26. On Cilicia, see Syme, *Buckler Studies* (1939) 299f. On Antonius' command, see *MRR* i 568–70. The details are not at all clear. One must here mention

the famous 'Pirate Law' found at Delphi in the 19th century, and not edited until 1921. (See *FIRA²*, no. 9, pp. 121f.) Like so many ancient documents, it survives only to taunt us with our ignorance. Though it looks as if it should fit into this general political context, it seems to be of 100; and nothing in our fairly abundant literature on that year had led anyone to expect it or, now that we have it, gives any real clue to its interpretation. There is no need to detail the gallant, but rather fanciful, attempts that have been made to explain it and assign it a place. (See *FIRA²*, l.c.)

27. On M. Antonius and his connections, see now *SGRH*, Index. Some scholars have questioned my conclusions from the evidence I cited; but I have so far found no reason to change my mind on any significant point. This is not the place to re-argue the matter. On Q. Catulus, see *SGRH* 37f. (with notes). The consuls cannot be dissociated from Antonius' extraordinary command: a point often forgotten.

28. All this is discussed in *FC*, ch. IX. For some of it, in greater detail, see *SGRH* 47f. (with notes). P. A. Brunt has now (*JRS* 1965, 106f.) denied that it was the censors of 97/6 who enrolled the Italians whose arrogation of citizenship gave rise to the *lex Licinia Mucia* of 95. He claims that 'the parallel of the expulsion of 187 suggests that it had been a gradual process'. I am afraid that, for once, I cannot understand or follow his argument. In 187 (or, for that matter, partly even in 177) there was no question of illegality in gaining citizenship: what the Latins asked for and achieved was the repatriation (in the physical sense) of the citizens they had lost, even though the loss had been perfectly legal (it seems). The Romans, in carrying out the expulsion of 187, based themselves on the census of 204/3 (Livy xxxix 3, 5), which was the first reasonably complete one for a long time (Livy xxix 37, 4f.: it also included, at Rome, a record of the citizens and property of the *duodecim coloniae*, which must have been a great help in 187). The movement had gone on for a long time simply because it was legal and no one thought of stopping it. By 177 (which Brunt omits to mention), things were already a little different. This time there *was* a complaint of illegality, and evidence of evasion by legal trickery. This time the base fixed was the censorship of 189/8 (i.e. of only twelve years before)—the year before the first decree had been passed. It is unlikely that the illegalities complained of had been connived at (or at least overlooked) by—of all men—the censors of 184/3, L. Flaccus and M. Cato, whose severity became proverbial. In fact, it was almost certainly the censors of 179/8—i.e. the last before the complaints—who were to blame in this case: they had reorganised the voting lists and introduced new criteria for tribal membership, as Livy tells us in a confused account that makes it clear he himself was copying out what he did not understand (xl 51, 9 'mutarunt suffragia regionatimque generibus hominum causisque et quaestibus tribus discripserunt'—see *JRS* 1962, 204f.). It was not surprising that some irregularities should have escaped notice in the reorganisation. However, though

suggestive, it is not really parallel to the phenomenon of the early nineties: the wholesale arrogation of citizenship by men who had no right to it. And it takes more faith than I can muster to believe (as Brunt's view implies) that masses of them invaded the citizen lists, or had this invasion confirmed, in the census *preceding* that of 97/6—i.e. that of 102/1, by two Metelli (*MRR* i 567), again noted for severity. Though any degree of complexity can always be substituted for the simplest explanation, it is more reasonable to draw the obvious conclusion from the close sequence of censorship and revision law than to go to extremes of paradox to avoid it.

29. Thrace (T. Didius): *MRR* i 571; Spain (M. Marius): *MRR* i 568; Sicily (C. Servilius): *ibid.*
30. See *op. cit.* (n. 14).
31. Diod. xxxvi 3.
32. For M. Annius, see *SIG*³ 700. In general, see now the useful collection of such honours (unfortunately without dates, even where they are known) in G. W. Bowersock, *Augustus and the Greek World* (1965) 150f.
33. Plut. *Sulla* 5.
34. *Mithr.* 11f.
35. See *SGRH* 45f. (with notes).
36. Sall. *hist.* iv 69, 5 and 22 M.
37. Plut. *Mar.* 36.
38. See W. Allen, *CP* 1938, 90f.; and *FC* 193.

CHAPTER V

1. Livy xlv 18, 3; see p. 18 above.
2. See Frank, *RI* 284f.
3. For this interpretation of L. Philippus as an extreme Optimate, co-operating with the Equites from common hostility to the reforms of M. Drusus, rather than from any positive community of interests, see R. Thomsen, 'Das Jahr 91 v. Chr. und seine Voraussetzungen', *C & M* v, 1942, 13f.
4. This was one of Gelzer's starting-points in the argument developed in *Die Nobilität der röm. Republik.*
5. If we may adapt a contemptuous phrase by an unknown officer of C. Caesar (*b. Afr.* 57) about a man serving in the opposing army.
6. The names and provenance of many of them can easily be gathered from *MRR*, together with such works as Syme, *The Roman Revolution*, and Taylor, *The Voting Districts of the Roman Republic.* The wealth of these circles is proclaimed by the records of their munificence surviving in innumerable inscriptions all over Italy. One of the (minor, it appears) duties of colonial aediles and duumvirs was the contribution of not less than 2 000 HS each towards the cost of games to Jupiter, Juno and Minerva

(*lex Urs.* lx 70–71=*FIRA* i 182–3). A duumvir of Sinuessa entertained the whole of the population of the colony (as well as that of a suburb, apparently not included in it) to *mulsum et crustum*, and the population of the colony as well as all his *gens* (all who would come along?) to dinner and gladiatorial games and put up a monument costing 12,000 HS, all (it seems) in honour of a dead relative (*ILLRP* ii 667).

7. This was noted particularly by Gabba, *Athenaeum* xliv, 1956, 124f.; this survey finally destroyed the myth of Sulla's hostility to the Equites as a class. See now also the same author's discussion in *ASNP* 1965, relating the programme of Sulla to that of M. Livius Drusus and his circle.

8. On the reform of 70, see *MRR* ii 127. (See now R. Rossi, *PP* 1965, 133; though I cannot accept the whole of his analysis of the 'groups' among the oligarchs.) On 106, see the frequent references by Cicero, collected Greenidge-Clay[2] 78. How long Caepio's law was in force is not certain: it depends on when we put the law of Glaucia, which seems to have superseded it. But this cannot be later than 100, since that was the year of Glaucia's death.

9. For an interesting study of the earlier period, see A. Alföldi, *Der frührömische Reiteradel und seine Ehrenabzeichen* (1952). Hill, *The Roman Middle Class* (1952), fails even to see the problem. I have attempted a brief sketch in *OCD*[2], s.v. 'Equites'. Nicolet has now partly filled the gap; see my comments in the Introduction.

10. See, e.g., A. Stein, *Der Römische Ritterstand* (1927) 23f. It should be added, as a minor qualification (insisted on by Stein), that free birth was a prerequisite, in normal times.

11. See Cic. *Q.fr.* i 1, 15; 18: 32f.; 2, 6; 10f.

12. See *RE*, s.v. 'Licinius' 104, col. 400; and cf. *MRR* ii 133, 139; 146.

13. *MRR* ii 169 (mid-63).

14. *ILLRP* i 370, 374, 376, 380, 387, 408; and many from Delos.

15. The story is told, not very clearly (since he wrote for people who probably knew the conditions), by the officer who wrote *b. Afr.* (87f.).

16. *Ibid.* 97 (note 'humilitas ciuitatis'); 36.

17. *b. Hisp.* 25f.

18. *Ibid.* 22.

19. *Ibid.* 31.

20. *SEHRE*[2] i 22f. (Quotation p. 24.)

21. On Roman settlement in these provinces, see now A. J. N. Wilson, *Emigration from Italy in the Republican Age of Rome*.

22. Memnon (*FgrHist* 434) 22. Others give different figures; but the extent of the massacre is, in general terms, not in doubt.

23. Cic. *imp. Cn. Pomp.* 18f.

24. I have discussed this province—from rather a different point of view—in *Mélanges Piganiol* (1966), 901f.

25. Cic. *Font.* 13f.

26. *Ibid.* 11; 46.
27. See pp. 19f. above.
28. See *MRR* ii 86. On border wars, see Chapter I above.
29. Caes. *b.c.* iii 9, 1.
30. This is recorded in an inscription that is not very accessible to the ordinary student. It was last published (to my knowledge) by Rendić-Miočević in *Studi Brusin* (1953), 67ff.
31. Caes. *b.c.* iii 29.
32. Frank, *Economic History of Rome*, 275f. (Similarly in *RI*.)
33. Rostovtzeff, *SEHHW* 870, was tempted, but (perhaps surprisingly) did not quite fall. He admits the motive of opening Syria to Roman businessmen as a secondary one.
34. R. Egger, *Die Stadt auf dem Magdalensberg* (1961). See Schleiermacher, *Gnomon* 1962, 316f.
35. Caes. *b.G.* iv 2.
36. *Rome beyond the Imperial Frontiers* (1954), 7.
37. See O. Brogan, *Roman Gaul* (1953), 132f. (wine-jars); cf. 143.
38. Caes. *b.G.* vii 3.
39. *Ibid.* i 1 'Belgae . . . a cultu atque humanitate prouinciae longissime absunt, minimeque ad eos mercatores saepe commeant.'
40. *SEHHW* 981 and n. 70.
41. See p. 54 above.
42. Asc. 57C.
43. *MRR* ii 145 and 150, n. 8. Cf. the SC mentioned in Cic. *Att.* i 19, 9, about which very little is known. (See Shackleton Bailey's note in his edition of Cic. *Att.* i and ii (1965), vol. i, p. 339.)
44. Mainly senators, of course, but not entirely: Atticus, at least, was expecting something of the sort to be done for him (Cic. *Att.* i 19, 9).
45. I have discussed this testament and tried to place it in its background in *RhM* 1967, 178f. Mr Michael Crawford tells me that he has noted exceptionally large issues of silver coinage in the middle 80s B.C.—which, in the *triennium sine armis*, seem surprising. The large amount of money collected from Tyre at this very time may have something to do with it.
46. See Cic. *l. agr.* ii 40f.
47. See (most conveniently) *RE*, s.v. 'Rabirius', no. 6.
48. This is given by Plutarch (*Pomp.* 45, apparently quoting, ultimately, Pompey's triumphal tablets) as 200 million HS.
49. The *pro Rabirio Postumo* survives, the *pro Gabinio*, which would have been at least equally interesting (in the light of what Cicero had said about the accused after his return from exile), unfortunately does not—perhaps for that very reason.
50. See the summary in Downey, *History of Antioch* 139f.
51. The former (a wild fancy) is Rostovtzeff's (*SEHHW* ii 870), the latter Downey's (l.c.).

52. *Viz.* Jews and Syrians (Cic. *prov. cons.* 10). This kind of intervention was rare and (as became clear) dangerous. The *lex Pompeia* of Bithynia-Pontus is amply attested in the tenth book of Pliny's *Letters.*

53. On this see *RE*, s.v. 'Licinius', no. 68, col. 314. For senators' shares in the tax companies, see Cic. *Vat.* 29 (*partes* held by Caesar—quite openly, it seems).

Chapter VI

1. Such as the *de imperio Cn. Pompei* and the *de provinciis consularibus* (the latter delivered in the Senate, but, in its published version, intended as a political pamphlet for wide circulation).

2. p. 36 above.

3. Particularly as Clodius apparently did not limit the number of recipients. This was done by Caesar during his reorganisation of the state. He fixed it at 150,000, reducing it by more than half (Suet. *Jul.* 41; Dio, xliii 21, *fin.*; Plut. *Caes.* 55; cf. Livy, *per.* cxv, apparently connecting the reduction with his policy of settling *proletarii* in overseas colonies).

4. On this and what follows, see my discussion in *JRS* 1965, 110f.

5. See Oost's perceptive study of Cato's personality and methods in *CP* 1955, 98f.

6. On Pompey's achievement in the East, see Gelzer, *Pompeius*[2] (1959), ch. VI; J. van Ooteghem, *Pompée le Grand* (1954), 244f. (the best summary). Pompey himself claimed to have founded 39 cities (Plut. *Pomp.* 45, 3).

7. On this, see my *FC* 88f.

8. *Ibid.* 74; cf. 114, with note 4.

9. Pliny, *n.h.* vii 99.

10. On this, see Jos. *ant.* xiv 74=*b.J.* i 154 (contrasting it with Syria, as not being under a Roman governor).

11. Plut. *Pomp.* 45. Plutarch's word for these revenues is τέλη, which is surely a translation of *uectigalia.* It must here refer to income from provinces, which alone is to the point. Drumann-Groebe, rather oddly, took it to refer to tariffs (iv 494).

12. Syme, *Rom. Rev.* 17.

13. This is discussed—though not always adequately—in all the standard works and does not need detailed documentation here. The sources are well collected in Greenidge-Clay[2] 211-22.

14. I have alluded to this aspect of Sulla's victory in *SGRH* 232. There is more to be said.

15. See pp. 56f. above.

16. On Cn. Pompeius Strabo the standard discussion is still Gelzer's epoch-making essay (now in his *Kl. Schr.* ii 106).
17. On this, see my discussion in *FC* 267f., 272f.; cf. *Hermes* 1955, 115.
18. For the figures, with evidence and discussion, see Drumann-Groebe iv 486f.; cf. Gelzer, *Pompeius*[2] 111 and 263, n. 243.
19. This, of course, is the background to the fear that Rome felt in the last years of Pompey's absence; though in fact he had no revolutionary designs. (On this principle in the interpretation of Pompey's aims and character, I fully agree with A. N. Sherwin-White, *JRS* 1956, 5–9; though I think it does not apply to the very beginning of his public career.)
20. The saying is variously quoted, e.g. Plut. *Cr.* 2; Cic. *off.* i 25. The most precise version (Pliny, *n.h.* xxxiii 134) deserves preference: 'nisi qui redditu annuo legionem tueri posset.'
21. For what follows, see Plut. *Cr.* 2.
22. For rates of pay at this time, see (with some caution!) Watson, *Historia* 1958, 113.
23. Val. Max. v 7, *ext.* 2.
24. Cic. *Att.* vi 1, 3; cf. 2,5.
25. Cic. *fam.* xiii 56 (see Tyrrell-Purser's note iii[2] 139).
26. Drumann-Groebe iv 479.
27. For a fitting commentary, see Tyrrell-Purser iii[2], pp. xxiif. and 337f. (with full references).
28. On this, see Oost, *CP* 1955, 98. It can hardly have been when he was quaestor in Cilicia under Appius (*vir. ill.* 82, 32).
29. Tyrrell-Purser iii[2], p. xxvi.
30. See Tyrrell-Purser iii[2], 339f. (citing Mommsen).
31. Cic. *Att.* vi 5, 5.
32. Cic. *Att.* v 21, 7.
33. See especially the useful collection of the evidence in R. O. Jolliffe, *Phases of Corruption in Roman Administration* (1918).
34. The story is told in Jos. *ant.* xiv 80f.
35. Zon. x 5.
36. Sydenham, *Coinage of the Roman Republic* (1952), nos. 912–4: Aretas kneeling, with camel and olive-branch with fillets (58 B.C.).
37. See Drumann-Groebe iv 467.
38. See pp. 55f. above: having made his prestige point, Sulla withdrew.
39. See *MRR* ii 215. Opposition in Rome (best known the curses of Ateius) was almost certainly due chiefly to antagonism to Crassus—and, in any case, was totally ineffective, bringing trouble upon the opponents.
40. Suet. *Jul.* 29 (also Paullus).
41. References Drumann-Groebe iii 345.
42. Plut. *Caes.* 29.
43. On these loans, see Cic. *Att.* vii 3, 11, with the notes in Tyrrell-Purser (iii[2] 306); 8, 5.

44. The phrase is Syme's (*CP* 1955, 137).
45. Cic. fam. vii 5–18. Cf. the judgment of Caelius (Cic. *fam.* viii 4, 2): 'qui solet infimorum hominum amicitiam sibi qualibet impensa adiungere.'
46. Sources in Gelzer, *Caesar*⁶ 264 (selection). C. Hirrus lent him 6,000 *murenae* for the banquet (Pliny, *n.h.* ix 171). Suetonius gives the sum distributed to the legionaries as 24,000 HS, Dio as 20,000.
47. Sherwin-White, *G & R* 1957, 36f.
48. See p. 78 above.
49. See Gelzer, *Caesar*⁶ 152, which Sherwin-White does not sufficiently consider. Caesar, in his Gallic triumph, claimed that over a million Gauls had died (Pliny, *n.h.* vii 92); the figure is given as a round one by Plutarch (*Caes.* 15, *fin.*), with the addition that as many were captured: probably this information also goes back to Caesar's triumph, as well as the claim that these enemy losses amounted to two thirds of all who had fought against him. Gelzer's statement that the country lost two thirds of all men able to bear arms rests on a misunderstanding of this claim. Still, the losses were heavy enough, if there is any truth whatever in these official figures. Gelzer also gives some useful figures to document the way in which Gaul had been drained of its resources: thus the price of gold seems to have suddenly fallen by a quarter! It is in the light of all these known facts that one must judge the 'clemency' of the Gallic settlement.
50. Gelzer, *op. cit.* 308. Cf. A. Heuss, *Röm. Gesch.* (1960) 208: 'Flucht in die Aussenpolitik.'
51. I had something to say about this in *FC*, e.g. 165f. It has now been carefully studied and abundantly documented in G. W. Bowersock, *Augustus and the Greek World* (1965).

INDEX OF NAMES

This Index includes both personal and geographical names, except (in general) those mentioned only once. Roman names are given under the *nomen* (except for the familiar 'Augustus'), with a cross-reference under the *cognomen* where necessary. Roman senators are identified, if consular, by the date of their consulship; if not, by the date of the highest regular office held. Only the first tenure is noted. Names of cities and countries include those of their inhabitants; e.g., for 'Italy' read, where appropriate, 'Italians'. 'Rome' (abbreviated 'R.' throughout) has not been indexed. The indexing of end notes, as usual, poses problems. In general, notes have been separately indexed only for items that would have been, if the note had been (where all notes ought to be) at the foot of the page: exceptions have been made in a few cases, to provide more information.

III

in debt to Pompey 82f., 86; in debt to Brutus 86

Aristonicus, Pergamene pretender fights against R. 22f.

Armenia 37f.; annexation not intended by Lucullus 39; and *see* Tigranes

Asia (province) 38; name 22f.; era 97[23]; first organised (corruptly) by Aquillius 48, 56; C. Gracchus' reform of tribute collection 47, 49f.; Scaevola sent to reorganise 10, 31, 48, 54; left by Pompey 'in heart of empire' 78; its tribute transforms empire 47f.; Italian interests in 66f., 69; basic to Roman economic activity 67; not always profitable for *publicani* 54, 75; distress of 31, 48, 63, 66, 79

Asia Minor 31f., 55; organisation after Syrian War 2; intervention by R. after war with Perseus 3; offered to Antiochus III as sphere of influence 7; mission of Scaurus to 32f., 42, 54; Lucullus in 37; Pompey's profits in 81, 90

Attalus III Philometor, King of Pergamum 97; leaves kingdom to R. 21f., 30f., 44f., 48, 77, 100[4]

Atticus *see* Pomponius

Augustus 89, 92, 93[1]

Aurelius Cotta, C. (*cos.* 75) concerned in organisation of Cyrene 35; in famine 36; disliked by Sallust 35f.

BITHYNIA 5, 38; occupied by Mithridates 56; made province by Pompey 75, 77, 83; Pompey's profits from this 83; keeps its name 23; and *see* Nicomedes

Brutus *see* Junius

CAECILIUS METELLUS NUMIDICUS, Q.

(*cos.* 109) 27, 32; popularity 51; trial 103[19]

Caesar *see* Julius

Calpurnius Piso Frugi, L. (*cos.* 133) passes first extortion law (149) 9, 41; opposes distribution of grain 46

Cappadocia 38; Bithynian and Pontic intrigues in 32; Marius meets Mithridates in 32; seized by Mithridates, 'freed' by R. 32f.; Ariobarzanes chosen King 33; Ariobarzanes installed by Sulla 33, 55f.; reoccupied by Mithridates and 'freed' by Aquillius 56; invaded by Mithridates (88) 57f.; Pompey its patron, to his profit 82; and *see* Ariobarzanes

Carthage 18, 47, 94[8]; left standing (201) 2; treaties with R. 5; purpose of destruction 20; annexation necessary after new war 9f.; C. Gracchus' colony at 24, 51f., 98[32]

Cato *see* Porcius

Cicero *see* Tullius

Cilicia 38, 75; command against pirates, established (102) with Marius' co-operation 52; territorial province after Servilius Vatia 35, 52; increased by Pompey 77; joined to Cyprus 77; Cicero its governor 82f., 86

Cirta Italians at 26, 70

Claudius Pulcher, C. (*cos.* 92) dedication to him at Cyrene 99[1]

Clodius Pulcher, P. (*aed.* 56) 85; grain law (58) and effects 76f.

Cornelii Scipiones aim at excessive *auctoritas* 8; epitaphs of 12

Cornelius Lentulus Marcellinus, Cn. (*cos.* 56) legate at Cyrene 36f.

Cornelius Lentulus Marcellinus, P. (*q.* 75 or 74) organises Cyrene 35f.; sent to find money for grain purchase 37

Cornelius Lentulus Spinther, P. (*cos.* 57) gives *lex prouinciae* to Cyprus 77; exploits Cyprus 87

Cornelius Scipio Africanus, P. (*cos.* 205) 23, 27; opposed to evacuation of Greece 2

Cornelius Scipio Africanus Aemilianus, P. (*cos.* 147) 19; at Numantia 25; patron of Jugurtha 25

Cornelius Scipio Asiaticus, L. (*cos.* 190) 8, 13, 23, 27

Cornelius Scipio Nasica, P. (*cos.* 162) opposes Cato on foreign policy(?) 4, 94[8]

Cornelius Scipio Nasica Serapio, P. (*cos.* 138) kills Ti. Gracchus 22; in charge of annexation of Pergamum 22

Cornelius Sulla, L. (*cos.* 88) 23, 36, 38, 52, 55f., 66, 88; instals Ariobarzanes 33; adlects 300 equites to Senate, creating link between orders 62; refuses to annex Egypt 31, 33f.; foreign policy not expansionist 31, 33f.; claims to have extended frontiers 34, 43, 76; effects of his rebellion 79f.

Cotta *see* Aurelius

Crassus *see* Licinius

Cyprus annexed and squeezed dry by Cato to provide money for grain distribution 76f., 87; joined to Cilicia, receives *lex* from Lentulus Spinther 77; extortion by governors before Cicero 87; Brutus' relations with 84f.

Cyrene 43; left to Rome (96) and exploited, but not organised 22, 29f.; no strong feelings over this 40f.; anarchy there seen by Lucullus 36; organised (75) to provide money for grain distribution 22, 30, 35f.; perhaps no permanent administration there before Pompey 36f.

DECIANUS *see* Appuleius

Delos Italians on 17, 60, 64, 70

Domitius Ahenobarbus, Cn. (*cos.* 122) settles Gaul without annexation 24 98[30]; his faction supports foundation of Narbo 24

Drusus *see* Livius

EGYPT 43, 102[8]; willed to Rome, but not annexed 31, 73; no strong feeling over this 40f.; not annexed by Sulla 31, 33f., 73; agitation for annexation in 60s 73f.; restoration of Ptolemy 'Auletes' to 73f.

Euphrates crossed by Lucullus 37, 39; and by Pompey 88

Europe 3; claimed by R. as sphere of influence 7

FALCIDIUS overbids for taxes of Tralles 47, 66

Flaccus *see* Valerius

Flamininus *see* Quinctius

Frank, Tenney rightly denies 'economic imperialism' in second century 19f., 70; wrongly asserts it in first century 70, 76

GABINIUS, A. (*cos.* 58) prohibits loans to foreigners 73; his law evaded by powerful men 84f.; restores Ptolemy 'Auletes' 74; interferes with *publicani* in Syria 75

Galba *see* Sulpicius

Gaul (Transalpine) 27, 39, 52, 56; not annexed after major war in 120s 23f.; organised after German wars 24, 29; prohibition of vine and olive culture in 19f., 68; no economic interest by R. before 100 24; Italian interests in, in first century 67f.; trade beyond province 71; Caesar's war in, with consequences 89f.

land in Gaul 67; reverses Lucullus' arrangements 38; founds colonies in East 52; his arrangements in East 77; secures vast increase in revenues, especially through client princes 78f.; arrangements in Syria 75; makes and breaks treaty with Parthia 88; profits of eastern campaigns 81; surpasses M. Crassus in wealth 82; Ariobarzanes' debt to him 82f.; opposition to him in R. 39; alleged representative of Equestrian imperialism 70; example to Crassus and Caesar 88f.

Pomponius Atticus, T. 20, 97[14]; pleads with Cicero to collect Brutus' debt 85; expects special dispensation from debt law 107[44]

Pontus plundered by Nicomedes IV for Roman benefit 51; annexation necessary after Mithridates' defeat 38; made province by Pompey 75, 77; and see Mithridates

Porcius Cato, C. (cos. 114) convicted 50

Porcius Cato ('Censorius'), M. (cos. 195) opposed by Scipio Nasica(?) 4; attacks Galba 10; trading interests 41

Porcius Cato ('Uticensis'), M. (pr. 54) 84; annexes Cyprus to pay for grain distribution 77; squeezes large sum out of Cyprus 77, 87; proposes Caesar's surrender to enemy 39

Ptolemy (VII) Euergetes ('Physcon'), King of Egypt wills kingdom to R. 97[19], 100[4]

Ptolemy (X) Alexander I, King of Egypt borrows from R. 73; in return, wills kingdom to R., but will not accepted 31, 73, 100[4]; acceptance urged by M. Crassus 73f.

Ptolemy (XI) Alexander II, King of Egypt sent to Egypt by Sulla 31, 100[4]

Ptolemy (XII) Neos Dionysos ('Auletes'), King of Egypt borrows to obtain recognition 73f.; expelled, borrows more for restoration 74f., 83; restored by Gabinius, appoints Rabirius finance minister 74

Ptolemy Apion, King of Cyrene leaves kingdom to R. 29f., 100[4]; and see Cyrene

Pulcher see Claudius, Clodius

Pyrrhus, King of Epirus war with R. 6

QUINCTIUS FLAMININUS, T. (cos. 198) policy of 'liberation' of Greece 2; confers with Antiochus III's envoys in Rome 7; discovers power of Greek public opinion 10

RABIRIUS POSTUMUS, C. (pr. 48?) agent for Ptolemy 'Auletes' 74, 83; defended by Cicero 74

Rhodes powerful after Syrian War 2; humiliated after war with Perseus 3

Rostovtzeff, M. 107[51]; on 'economic imperialism' in second century 19f., 70, 96[1]; on 'hegemonial imperialism' 94[9]; on enfranchisement of Italy 65; on R. and Syria 71, 107[33]

Rullus see Servilius

Rutilius Rufus, P. (cos. 105) on Marius 99[49]; prosecution of 42, 50

SALAMIS, city on Cyprus in debt to Brutus 84f., 87

Sallustius Crispus, C. (= 'Sallust') (pr. 46), historian 27, 35f., 51; biased on Jugurthine War 25, 27; dislikes C. Cotta 35f.

Sardinia 4; made prouincia 8

Saturninus *see* Appuleius

Scaevola *see* Mucius

Scaptius, M. Brutus' financial agent 84f.

Scaurus *see* Aemilius

Scipio *see* Cornelius

Sempronius Gracchus, C. (*tr. pl.* 123) 25, 40, 54; extortion law 41; scheme of administrative reform 45f., 49f., 102[12]; its breakdown 50f.; his colony at Carthage 24, 51f., 98[32]; establishes People's right to profit by empire 36, 44f., 48f., 76, 79; implications of this for provinces 46; pushed to conclusion by Clodius and Pompey 76f.; establishes power of Equites 50, 60; 'makes state two-headed' 26, 61, 99[43]

Sempronius Gracchus, Ti. (*tr. pl.* 133) 25, 30, 40, 51, 54, 95[31], 97[21]; uses Attalus' bequest for his plans 21f., 44f.; asserts People's right to profit by empire 36, 44f., 49, 76f.

Servilius Caepio, Q. (*cos.* 106) fails to reconcile Senate and Equites 62

Servilius Rullus, P. (*tr. pl.* 63) land bill of 77

Servilius Vatia, P. (*cos.* 79) Isaurian conquests of 35

Sicily 23, 52; made *prouincia* 8; probably profitable for R. 8, 18, 47f.; 'free' allies left there 6; extra grain purchased there 36; slave war in 53

Spain 24, 67; wild tribal frontier 4, 54; maladministration in (171) 8; cruelty and perfidy in R.'s wars in 10, 90 (and *see* Sulpicius Galba); fighting in (*c.* 100) 53; Sertorius in 36; in Civil War 64f.

Sulla *see* Cornelius

Sulpicius Galba, Ser. (*cos.* 144) attacked by Cato 10; not punished for mass murders in Spain 10, 95[23f.]; becomes honoured orator 10

Syria returned to Seleucids by Lucullus 39, 70; annexation by Pompey not due to Equites 70f.; due to traditional reasons 74f., 77; Pompey's tax arrangements there 75; M. Scaurus in 87f.; M. Crassus' province 88f.

TIGRANES I ('the Great'), King of Armenia 39, 88

Tralles, city of Asia 47, 66

Transalpina *see* Gaul

Tullius Cicero, M. (*cos.* 63) 1, 47, 53, 67, 69, 74, 79, 86f., 89, 97[14]; arouses sympathy for Roman clients against foreigners 9; on prohibition of vine and olive culture in Gaul 19f., 68; on C. Gracchus 45f.; on importance of Asia 47, 67; praises Equestrian juries 50; on rise of non-noble to consulship 61; advice to brother in Asia 63; attests power of provincial Romans 63f.; on confiscations in Gaul 67; opposes Rullus' bill 77; in Cilicia, involved in debts owed to Pompey and Brutus 82f.; social background to his *concordia ordinum* 62f.

Tullius Cicero, Q. (*pr.* 62), brother of preceding receives advice on provincial government from his brother 63

VALERIUS FLACCUS, L. (*cos.* 100) in censorship (97/6) freely enrols Italians 53, 104[28]

Valerius Flaccus, L. (*pr.* 63) governs Asia 47

Verres, C. (*pr.* 74) 86f.; consuls (72) try to curb his maladministration in Sicily 10, 95[28]